MIXING AND MASTERING WITH CUBASE

Matthew Loel T. Hepworth

Hal Leonard Books
An Imprint of Hal Leonard Corporation

Published in 2012 by Hal Leonard Books
An Imprint of Hal Leonard Corporation
7777 West Bluemound Road
Milwaukee, WI 53213

Trade Book Division Editorial Offices
33 Plymouth St., Montclair, NJ 07042

Printed in the United States of America

Book design by Adam Fulrath
Book composition by Rainbow Tiger Design

Library of Congress Cataloging-in-Publication Data

Hepworth, Matthew Loel T.
   Mixing and mastering with Cubase / Matt Loel T. Hepworth.
     p. cm.
   Includes index.
   ISBN 978-1-4584-1367-3
1. Cubase. 2. Digital audio editors. I. Title.
   ML74.4.C8H45 2012
   781.3'4536—dc23
                                                              2012017845

www.halleonardbooks.com

Mixing and Mastering with Cubase

quick **PRO**
guides

CONTENTS

Chapter 1

Chapter 2

Chapter 5

Chapter 6

Chapter 7

Chapter 8

PREFACE

Editing, Mixing, and Mastering (Oh My)

As much as I love the recording process, the editing, mixing, and mastering processes, while typically more laborious, are equally exciting. Every musician or performer has poured his or her heart and soul into the tracks he or she has recorded. But the music can't effectively communicate to the listener without the mixing that makes it speak as one voice, one idea, or one message. Proper and appropriate editing, mixing, and mastering can make or break the effectiveness of a piece of music. As the author, it is my goal to empower you with the knowledge and skill to better communicate to your or your client's end listeners.

What Happens During the Mix, Stays in the Mix

At the 1988 Winter NAMM (National Association of Music Merchants) show, I went to a concert featuring one of the best-known and most admired drummers of the modern era. That drummer will remain nameless, but during the setup and sound check, he continually berated and insulted the monitor engineer, who I could tell was genuinely trying to accommodate the demands of each band member. This continued throughout the concert, until the engineer reached his breaking point. As the drummer screamed at him red-faced from behind the drum set, the engineer stood motionless, arms folded, refusing to provide any further accommodation. No one else in the band had monitor problems, which proved he was competent and dedicated. I learned a valuable lesson that night: don't be mean to the engineer, for he or she has the power to make you sound good . . . or bad.

But live sound is very different from studio recording. That drummer went to a different town and a different venue with a different monitor engineer, so the bad sound (real or imagined) only lasted one night. But in the studio, whether it's your music or that of a client, what makes it onto the final product will be a permanent record of the music. Therefore, it is important to make the right choices during the mix. If issues or treatments are neglected or done improperly, the results will be forever audible.

Bending or Breaking the Rules of Mixing

Mixing, like any art form, becomes boring when rules make it impossible to push the envelope. Therefore, there are only a handful of unbreakable rules. I'll be putting emphasis on those rules (such as not exceeding 0 dB) throughout the book. But you should also feel free to explore other ways of achieving your own sound, rules or not.

For example, I was talking with Grammy award–winning engineer/producer Francis Buckley about his mixing work on Alanis Morissette's *Jagged Little Pill* album. He mixed the song "Perfect," and I asked him how he made the vocals sound so organic and intimate, to which he replied, "Well, I didn't use a compressor." My befuddled response went something like, "Wow, no compressor on the vocals? Really? That's almost unheard of. How'd you think of that?" His next response spoke volumes (pun intended) about his level of mixing maturity: "I listened to her vocal track, and it didn't need it." I nearly had to sit down. To realize that he listened first, considered the options, then threw out the rule book and achieved fantastic results really affected my own approach to mixing. That's the day I started relying more on my ears than my past experience or convention. I would urge you to use the same approach. Bend or break the breakable rules, and listen carefully to the results. You might be pleasantly surprised.

Dreaming of Digital

Let me take you back to February of 1984. Once strictly reserved for classical music, audio CDs of pop music were just hitting the record store shelves. As a fan of Peter Gabriel, I was thrilled to repurchase the CD version of his fourth album, known in the United States as *Security*. (For those of you in the know: yes, it is a West German "Target" disc.) As I stood at the checkout counter holding the shrink-wrapped package in my hands, I noticed a small, pink band on the cover artwork that read, "Full Digital Recording." This was the first time I'd ever seen such a listing. It meant the music was digitized into a series of numbers, and only when the consumer played the CD was it reconstructed into an analog signal. I couldn't fully grasp the concept, but it piqued my interest in recording music digitally.

It wasn't until I got home (CD players didn't appear in cars until late 1984) and listened to the CD that I started to understand the advantages of digital. First and foremost, there were no tape noise artifacts. Since the multitrack recording was done with a digital recorder, there was none of the ubiquitous tape hiss that we'd all put up with for so long. Next, my amplifier and speakers were challenged by the upper limits of the dynamic range. Yet the quiet passages revealed subtleties once reserved only for those who could afford the most esoteric and expensive of phonographs. I thought to myself, "Someday I'll be able to make my own digital recordings."

"Someday" Only Took Eight Years

Throughout most of the '80s and '90s, I worked in music stores, selling keyboards and recording equipment. It was a great way to learn about the newest digital technology, and it left my nights free to play gigs. In 1992, we received our first shipments of a new product from Alesis known as the ADAT (Alesis Digital Audio Tape). It was the world's first affordable digital 8-track recorder. Suddenly, for just under $4,000, musicians and engineers alike could own a digital multitrack recording device. To say that it revolutionized the project- and home-studio market would be an understatement.

While it was the first, and therefore most affordable, digital multitrack recorder on the market, I still needed a mixer, compressors, effect processors, and a 2-track DAT machine to mix down to. I also needed boxes of cables and S-VHS tape stock with which to feed the ADATs. While the ADAT made the dream of the digital home-recording studio a reality, it was still an expensive proposition.

The Dawn of the DAW

Music software has been around ever since the early '80s. In fact, I still have the music cartridges that in 1982 allowed me to sequence music on my Commodore 64 even before there was MIDI. (I still use my Commodore 64 computers with the MSSIAH MIDI cartridge from 8bitventures.com.) But in 1993, Steinberg released Cubase Audio. It allowed Atari Falcon (computer) owners to run Cubase MIDI tracks and up to eight digital Audio tracks simultaneously. I had been using Steinberg Pro16 MIDI sequencing software on my Commodore 64 for years, but didn't get into Cubase Audio until it became available on Windows in 1996. Together with my Yamaha CBX-D5 and CBX-D3 audio interfaces, I could play back just as many tracks as with my 8-track ADAT.

Time Becomes Nonlinear

Cubase Audio also allowed me to use the same digital editing techniques I'd been using on MIDI tracks for years. Suddenly I could cut, copy, and paste audio data from within the Cubase timeline. This kind of editing was unheard of on the ADAT because of its tape-based format, which rendered its timeline linear. Not only did Cubase Audio allow me to move audio data around the timeline as easily as I could with MIDI data, it also did it nondestructively. In other words, all of the original versions of my Audio tracks were retained on the hard drive. The price of this computer-based system was even less than the ADAT technology.

The Real World Becomes Virtual with VST

Later in 1996, Steinberg created VST, or Virtual Studio Technology. VST created virtual signal processors (such as EQ, compressors, chorus, and reverb effects) right inside of the computer. My gigantic mixer and racks of external signal processors were quickly becoming obsolete. Within a few years, Steinberg added VSTi, or VST Instruments, to Cubase that created virtual synthesizers, samplers, and drum machines inside of the computer. At that point, my synthesizers and samplers were getting obsolete too. Fortunately, this was also when eBay hit the scene, and I used it to sell off my hardware.

Cubase Is a Complete Recording Studio

Fast-forward to present day, and Cubase has become an entire recording studio right inside of your computer. Sure you'll still need mics, MIDI and audio interfaces, a few cables, instruments, speakers, and inspiration to make it all happen. But never before has the recording studio been more accessible to musicians and music enthusiasts alike. Consider this: Cubase LE and AI (limited editions of Cubase that ship with many third-party hardware products, Steinberg products, and Yamaha products) provide at least sixteen audio tracks. That's four times as many tracks as the Beatles ever had! We really do live in exciting times.

Be Careful What You Wish For

Now that you have an entire recording studio in your computer, learning how to use all of it can be a daunting task. Imagine you just walked into a state-of-the-art commercial recording facility and noticed all the buttons, switches, knobs, cables, and hardware that filled the control room. Now imagine you have to sit in the "big chair" and take charge of a recording session. Are you ready to do that? My guess is that you'd be besieged by the prospect of being thrown into the role of engineer and running all of that gear.

Well by purchasing Cubase and running it on your computer, you *are* sitting in the big chair. I've had the advantage of gradually experiencing the digital revolution throughout its various stages. But if in 1984 I'd been thrown into a recording studio and told to record music, I'd be completely overwhelmed and intimidated. I imagine that's how you feel right now. It might even be the reason you are reading this book.

How to Use This Book

I have faith that you will be able to become an accomplished Cubase user and do things I could only dream of doing back in 1984. But to do so, I recommend that you learn Cubase as you would a new musical instrument. Many of you play some sort of musical instrument. Unless you are a prodigy, wrangling the first notes out of the instrument didn't meet world-class standards. However, through daily practice and learning from mistakes, you became a competent musician. Or at the very least, you've learned enough to allow the instrument and the music you make with it to enrich your life.

If you apply that same approach to learning Cubase, you will be able to record your music (or the music of others) on your computer in the comfort of your home, project studio, or commercial facility. To say that Cubase and digital music production have irrevocably augmented my musical experience, as well as provided me with countless positive experiences, would be an understatement. I truly want you to have similar experiences with Cubase. It can happen for you if you practice each day, take breaks when overwhelmed, learn from your mistakes, and revel in your accomplishments. The music you make can enrich not only your life but also the lives of others. It can provide you with not only a creative outlet and/or a paycheck, but a living, and it has the potential to change the world. When all is said and done, it will leave a legacy of your time on Earth. Music has that power. But like so many other of life's experiences, it is better when shared with others.

With all that in mind, roll up your sleeves, take a deep breath, and open your mind and heart to the opportunities the digital age has to offer you.

Acknowledgments

I'd like to thank Karl Steinberg and Manfred Rürup for having the vision and courage to create such revolutionary products.

Thanks to Bill Gibson and everyone at Hal Leonard for bringing me into this project. Thanks also to copy editor Joanna Dalin Sexton for making the book readable. Together, they all made it a joy to create this book and bring the information to you.

Thanks to Alan Macpherson, Brian McGovern, and Greg Ondo at Steinberg North America, and Melanie Becker at Steinberg Media Technologies GmbH. Every author should be lucky enough to have the support of such wonderful people.

I would like to thank my parents— my "executive producers"—Connie Jo M. Hepworth-Woolston and the late Dr. Loel T. Hepworth, for recognizing the autodidact in me and providing an environment in which I could flourish.

This book is dedicated to my sister, Jillian Sabina Hepworth-Clark. I find solutions through your thoughtful wisdom, while your kindness and love bring me peace. You are my touchstone and my champion and I'm so fortunate to have you in my life.

MIXING AND MASTERING WITH CUBASE

Chapter 1

EDITING IN THE PROJECT WINDOW

If I were writing this book twenty-five years ago, this chapter on editing would be very short. That's because there was very little editing that could be done. Audio recording was taking place on open-reel analog tape decks. And other than the cutting and splicing of the analog magnetic tape with a (properly demagnetized) razor blade, the format simply didn't offer much else in the way of editing. But when technology gave way to digital recorders and ultimately DAW (Digital Audio Workstation) programs such as Cubase, the editing process exploded with an ever-expanding palette of creative and practical tools. Or in a more Cubase-specific sense, editing is the moving and rearranging of events in the Event Display of the Project window.

It's also important to know that with very few exceptions, any edits you make while you're in the Project window are nondestructive. Removing MIDI events can result in permanent erasure. That's one reason I rely on the Mute tool, which you'll learn about later in this chapter. However, with Audio events, you can cut, copy, and paste to your heart's content and never lose the original recording. In this chapter, we'll be exploring the basic editing concepts shared by MIDI, Instrument, and Audio tracks, including:

- Methods for the Cut, Copy, and Paste commands.
- The Toolbar and how it pertains to editing.
- The editing tools in the Toolbox.
- The Status, Info, and Overview lines.
- Zooming the Event Display.

More Than Cut, Copy, and Paste

One of the most amazing and useful functions of early computers was the ability to cut, copy, and paste (CCP) data within one document or into another. Undo and Redo were and are a fantastic remedy for those "oops" moments. Any of you who ever used a typewriter know what I'm talking about. I'll never forget the aggravation of making an irreparable mistake at the end of a page and having to start all over again, or the elation I felt when my mom bought an IBM Correcting Selectric II typewriter with the "last character erase" feature. Lest we forget, typewriters didn't autocorrect ourr speling errors, ether.

When sequencing programs allowed composers to record music in the 1980s, CCP opened a new world of creative and time-saving possibilities. Then in the 1990s, that same functionality could be performed on audio data as well. Today, the CCP commands are ubiquitous in practically all software programs, including Cubase. They're usually located in the Edit menu, which is where you'll find them in Cubase. However, the tools found in the Toolbar of Cubase go far beyond the basic CCP commands. That's not to say that CCP commands aren't useful, but I'm sure you'll see that the tools offer many more possibilities.

Basics for Cut, Copy, and Paste

If you're accustomed to relying on CCP commands, let me take a moment to discuss how they work in Cubase. For cut and copy commands, you must use the Object Selection tool, Range Selection tool, or other select command to define the events you'll be cutting or copying. (See "Object Selection Tool" and/or "Range Selection Tool" later in this chapter.) To paste the data you've cut or copied, you must both select the track and move the cursor to the temporal location to define the coordinates of the paste to occur.

Exploring the Toolbar

The Toolbar is located at the top of the Cubase Project window and is not visible unless you have started a new project or loaded an existing one. Hopefully, you've been doing a lot of recording and have plenty of material upon which to edit. If not, you can load the project titled "The Right Track Matt R02.cpr," located on the disc that accompanies this book. (See appendix A, "Using the Included Disc.")

Locating the Toolbar

You can find the Toolbar at the topmost margin of the Cubase Project window, as seen in Figure 1.1.

Figure 1.1: The Cubase Toolbar

You should already be familiar with some of the items on the Toolbar, including the Transport controls and Snap functions. But now that you're going to edit your material, we'll need to go over the Toolbox and the editing tools it contains.

The Toolbox is divided into several icons that depict their operation. Some tools have different operating modes, indicated by a small, white triangle that will appear when the tool is selected. For example, the Object Selection tool in Figure 1.2 is in a selected state, and the Mode indicator is shown at the bottom.

Figure 1.2: The Toolbox and Mode indicator

Selecting the Tools

You can select a tool at any time simply by clicking on its corresponding icon in the Toolbox. However, there are more and even faster ways to select tools. For example, you can Right/Ctrl-click in the Event Display to reveal an additional and identical Toolbox, as seen in Figure 1.3.

Figure 1.3: Right-/Ctrl-clicking in the Event Display

While holding the mouse button down, you simply drag your mouse to the right, hover over the tool you wish to use, and release the mouse button.

My favorite method is to use the top row of number buttons on the computer keyboard. In Figure 1.4, you'll see how the number keys correspond to the tools.

Typing the number key will select the corresponding tool. For example, typing the "3" key will select the Split tool. Typing the "1" key will select the Object Selection tool. However, repeatedly typing the "1" key will cycle through the three modes of the Object Selection tool.

You'll also notice that there are twelve tools, but only nine can be accessed by the number keys, and they're not selected concurrently. That's because some of the tools have more specialized functions. So you might wonder why Steinberg didn't group the specialized tools together in the Toolbox. The reason was to maintain the number-key-to-tool behavior that Cubase users have used for years. (Old timers, like me, rejoice!)

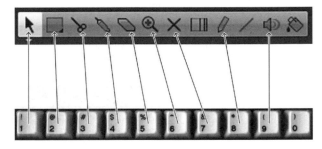

Figure 1.4: Corresponding number keys and tools

Tool Behavior and the Snap Settings

The behavior of the tools is highly influenced by the Snap settings. When Snap is off, the events and edits can be made freely at any temporal position. When Snap is on, the edits and movements made with the tools are constrained based upon the Snap settings in Figure 1.5.

Figure 1.5: The Snap settings

Snap can be turned on and off by clicking the Snap button or by typing the "J" key on your computer keyboard. For this chapter, the Snap type should be set to the default of Grid. The Grid type can be set to varying degrees of constraint, depending upon how fine a control is desired. For example, the default of Bar will constrain the edits to the bar lines of the Event Display. A setting of Beat will constrain the edits to the quarter-note resolution of the Event Display.

If an even finer degree of control is desired, setting the Grid type to Use Quantize will allow you to define the constraint based upon the Quantize Preset. For example, selecting the Quantize Preset of 1/16 (16th notes) will constrain the edits to the 16th-note resolution of the Event Display.

Temporarily Disabling Snap

If you find yourself making a series of edits and want to quickly disable Snap, you can hold down the Ctrl/Command key while making the edits. When you release the Ctrl/Command key, the Snap behavior will be reengaged.

Using the Tools

Each of the twelve tools in the Toolbox has a specific function. That functionality is only applicable to the events in the Event Display. For example, if you select the Split tool, the mouse icon will resemble the scissors icon, but only when the mouse is moved to the Event Display. When you move the mouse to any other region of the Cubase Project window, the mouse returns to its default "pointer" appearance. That allows you to see which tool you have selected during editing but leave the default appearance for other mouse operations outside of the Event Display.

The tools also make appearances in other editors, such as the Key and Drum Editors. Their functionality is virtually identical no matter which editor you're using them in. As we'll see in some of the subsequent chapters, the other editors offer a finer degree of detail. For now, let's go over each of the tools as they appear in the Toolbox from left to right, as shown in Figure 1.6.

Figure 1.6: The tools in the Toolbox

Object Selection Tool (Normal Sizing Mode)

The Object Selection tool in Normal Sizing mode is the default and most commonly used tool in the Toolbox. With it, you can click on events to select them. Selected events will turn black, making it easy to identify selected versus unselected events, as shown in Figure 1.7.

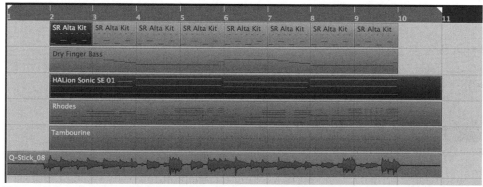

Figure 1.7: Selected and unselected events

Object Selection with the Shift Key

Shift-clicking and/or Ctrl/Command-clicking allows you to select multiple events.

You can also select a series of events by clicking and dragging from an empty area across several events, even across multiple tracks, as shown in Figure 1.8.

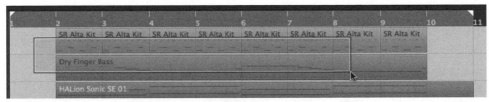

Figure 1.8: Click-and-dragging from an empty area

If you want to select several events that aren't surrounded by empty area, hold the Shift key while clicking and dragging, as shown in Figure 1.9.

Figure 1.9: Shift-clicking and dragging

Making Drag Copies

When you hover over an event and press the Alt/Option key, the Object Selection tool icon will turn into a small scissors pointing at a box. Clicking on an event (or series of selected events) while holding the Alt/Option key will create copies of the events that you can drag to different temporal locations, as shown in Figure 1.10.

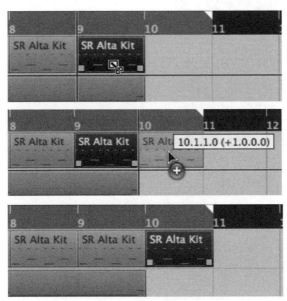

Figure 1.10: Drag copy before, during, and after

During the drag, a small "+" sign will appear underneath the mouse icon to indicate that you are making a copy. (That "+" sign has a square, clear background on Windows and a round, green background on a Mac.) If you want to make a drag copy and you forgot to hold the Alt/Option key prior to the drag, you can hold Alt/Option before releasing the mouse button to complete the drag copy operation.

You can also hold the Shift key along with Alt/Option to make a Shared copy. Any editing you make on that event will be reflected in all the events with which it is shared. (See "Making Shared Event Repeats" later in this chapter.)

Resizing Events

When you hover your mouse over an event, the Event Handles will appear, as shown in Figure 1.11.

Figure 1.11: The Event Handles

Clicking on the handles and dragging left or right allows you to resize the event. Audio events can be resized to the extent of their contents. In other words, if an Audio event was originally thirty seconds long, you could shorten it to any size. However, you could not extend the length to longer than thirty seconds.

Making Event Repeats

Another highly useful technique is to hold the Alt/Option button while dragging the right handle. When you hover the mouse over the handle while holding Alt/Option, the mouse icon turns into a pencil similar to the Draw tool icon. Clicking and dragging then creates Event Repeats, as shown in Figure 1.12.

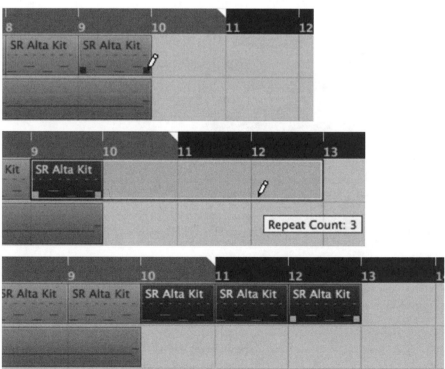

Figure 1.12: Creating Event Repeats

Be aware that each Event Repeat is independent of the original. This allows you to make further edits to the data without altering the original from which it was made. However, Shared Repeats work differently.

Making Shared Event Repeats

Shared Repeats allow you to make edits to one Shared Event, and all Shared Repeats will reflect the same edit. For example, if you edited the MIDI notes on a Shared Event to play the cowbell instead of the snare drum, all the Shared Repeats will also play cowbell. (Insert your own "more cowbell" joke here.) The process of making Shared Repeats is identical to that of making Event Repeats; you just hold down the Shift key in addition to the Alt/Option key during the drag, as shown in Figure 1.13.

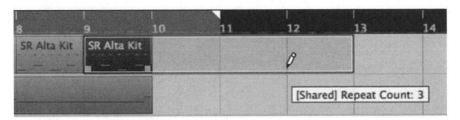

Figure 1.13: Creating Shared Event Repeats

Shared Events will also display a small "=" icon in their upper right-hand corner.

Other Object Selection Tool Modes

By default, the Object Selection tool is in Normal Sizing mode. When you alter the size of an event by dragging its handles, the data contained within the event is not altered. The data may get truncated when making an event smaller, but the remaining data is unaffected.

When you click on the Object Selection tool in the Toolbox, a submenu will appear and display the other two modes, as shown in Figure 1.14.

Figure 1.14: Object Selection tool modes

You can choose a different mode either by selecting it from the submenu or by repeatedly typing "1" on your computer keyboard (see Figure 1.4) to cycle through all three modes. Pay attention to the tool icon, as it depicts how the Object Selection tool will appear in the Event Display.

Using the Object Selection tool in these other modes is identical to resizing events. However, the results are quite different. Sizing Moves Contents will move the data contained within the event. Sizing Applies Time Stretch will keep all the data within the event, but apply time compression/expansion to alter the tempo of the event. Depending on the amount of the resizing, the sonic quality of the time stretch will vary slightly on Audio events. MIDI data, on the other hand, will retain its original sonic quality, because MIDI is not sound. The notes are simply placed at different temporal locations.

Range Selection Tool

The Range Selection tool is very useful for editing, copying, or deleting events across multiple tracks, and especially when the events have differing sizes. For example, Figure 1.15 shows events with both MIDI and Audio data and of varying sizes. If you wanted to remove all of the data between measures 5 and 7 across all the tracks, you would use the Range Selection tool to click and drag around that range.

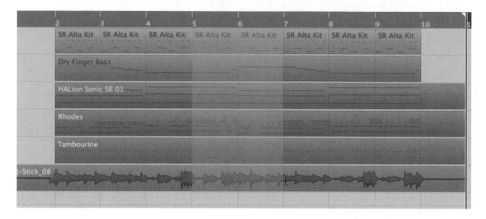

Figure 1.15: The Range Selection process

The range will appear as an opaque blue box to reveal the selected data. To erase the data within the range, type the Delete key on your keyboard, and the result will appear as it does in Figure 1.16.

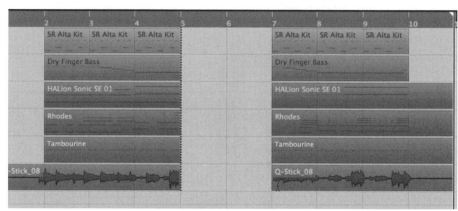

Figure 1.16: The range after the delete process

Notice that the deletion of the range resulted in the creation of more events. The lower tracks used to have one long event. But after the deletion of the range, there are now two events: one preceding and one following the range.

Other Range Selection Procedures

For these functions to work, you must first use the Range Selection tool to define the range. (See Figure 1.15.) When you hover your mouse over a selected range, the mouse icon will appear as a hand. Clicking and dragging the range will move the data to a new location and leave a gap similar to that in Figure 1.16. Holding Alt/Option while dragging will create a copy of the range while leaving the original range intact. (Note: Shared copies cannot be created with the Range Selection tool.)

Split Tool

The Split tool appears as a scissors and is the modern equivalent of using a razor blade on analog tape. That is, it splits one event into two events, or multiple events into many more events. For example, the Audio event in Figure 1.17 (Q-Stick_08) is one large event. If you want to split it into two separate events, use the Split tool to click on the event at the desired location.

Other Split Procedures

You can use the Split tool on a series of events, as long as they are selected first. For example, Figure 1.18 shows two selected events that are not vertically contiguous. But using the Object Selection tool and Shift-clicking each event will select them both. Then clicking with the Split tool will split both events.

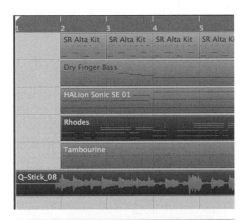

Figure 1.18: Using the Split tool across multiple events

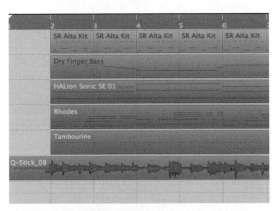

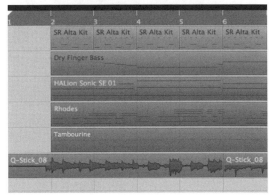

Figure 1.17: The Split procedure

Similarly, if you want to use the Split tool across all of the events, use the Select All command (Ctrl/Command A) to select all the events. Then click with the Split tool on any event and at the desired location.

Glue Tool

The Glue tool is the antithesis of the Split tool. Rather than making many from one, it makes one from many. It resembles a small tube of glue and is the digital equivalent of adhesive tape. When using the Glue tool on single events, it has a "left to right" behavior. In other words, clicking on an event will glue the next event to the right. That's true even if there is a void area between the events. Because of this left-to-right behavior, clicking on a right-most event (or a solitary event on a track) with the Glue tool will not produce any result. Figure 1.19 depicts the operation of the Glue tool.

Figure 1.19: Operation of the Glue tool

Other Glue Procedures

Another important behavior is that the Glue tool only works one track at a time and across like data. The latter is easy to understand, because you cannot glue MIDI events together with Audio events. However, the former means you cannot glue the events from one track to another. You could use the Object Selection tool, Range Selection tool, or Select All command to select multiple events. Then clicking with the Glue tool will join right events to the left events but keep the events relative to their original tracks.

Erase Tool

This is perhaps the most basic of the tools. It resembles the eraser used on chalkboards. Clicking on an event with the Erase tool will erase it from the Event Display.

Other Erase Procedures

You can erase multiple events across multiple tracks by first selecting the events with the Object Selection tool. You can also use the Range Selection tool to define a range of events, and then click on the range (opaque blue area, see Figure 1.15) to erase the contents. Additionally, you can hold Alt/Option while clicking on an event. Doing so erases all the events to the right but leaves the clicked event intact.

Zoom Tool

The normal behavior of the Zoom tool is as a horizontal zoom-in tool. Clicking and dragging over events with the Zoom tool will zoom in to reveal finer details. Clicking and dragging while holding Ctrl/Command will also zoom all tracks heights as well as zooming the events. I don't use the Zoom tool very often. But when I do, I like to keep the Overview line (see "The Status, Info, and Overview Lines" later in this chapter) visible so that I can use it to zoom out. There are additional provisions for zooming the Event Display that I'll go over later in this chapter.

Mute Tool

This is an extraordinarily powerful, yet misunderstood, tool. But after I describe how it works, you'll find yourself using it more and more. You see, when you remove MIDI events from the Event Display, they're gone forever. That is, unless you use the Undo command to restore them. But after you close the project, the MIDI events are unrecoverable. Audio events are quite different, because Cubase always remembers every audio recording you make in a special place called the Pool. Space constraints won't allow us to discuss the Pool in this book, so for now, let's learn how to use the Mute tool.

When you click on an event with the Mute tool, it gets grayed out and will not be audible during playback. So why not just delete the event with the Erase tool or by typing the Delete key on your keyboard? Because a muted event can be unmuted, thereby leaving it in place. Simply click on the muted event with the Mute tool, and it will become audible again during playback. This is perfect for when you think, "I don't want to use that event," but you change your mind later on.

The Mute tool resembles an "X." When you click on an event with the Mute tool, it will become grayed out and inaudible during playback, as shown in Figure 1.20.

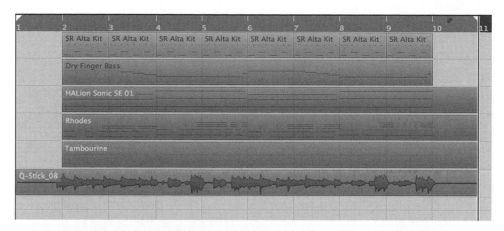

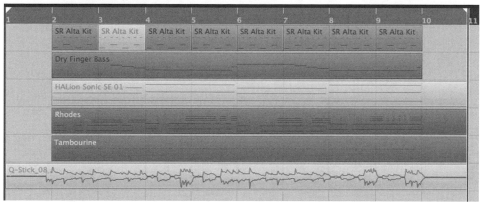

Figure 1.20: Operation with the Mute tool

Other Mute Procedures

You can mute multiple events by using the Object Selection tool or Select All command prior to Shift-clicking one of them with the Mute tool. You can also click and drag across multiple events to mute a range of events.

Time Warp Tool

Due to space constraints, the Time Warp tool will won't be covered in this book. Suffice it to say you cannot use the Time Warp tool to create clichéd plots for television and cinema.

Draw Tool

The Draw tool resembles a pencil and can be used to create blank events. This is especially useful on MIDI and Instrument tracks when you want to create new data in the Key, List, or Score editors. While you can create empty Audio events, there isn't much facility to use or edit them. The Draw tool can only be used on a track-by-track basis. In other words, you cannot create multiple events across multiple tracks.

Line Tool

The Line tool will be covered in appendix B, "A Primer on Automation."

Play Tool

The Play tool resembles a speaker and can be used to listen to individual events in the Event Display. It has two modes, and its operation will differ on MIDI or Audio events.

Play Tool in Play Mode

Clicking and holding on any MIDI or Audio event will start playback from the click location. Only the clicked event will be audible, and playback will adhere to the project tempo. If playback proceeds past the boundary of the clicked event, no sound will be produced by subsequent events. If you'd like to hear those events, click and hold on them with the Play tool in Play mode.

Play Tool in Scrub Mode

Scrubbing is a term that comes from the days of reel-to-reel analog tape. With the playback head engaged, you could manually wind the reels back and forth to listen closely for edit points. That's exactly how Scrub mode works, but be aware that it only works on Audio events. Click and hold the Play tool over an Audio event, and drag the mouse slowly from left to right. Then drag right to left. The speed of the scrubbing will depend on how quickly or slowly you're dragging the mouse. It even sounds like old analog tape going forward and backward.

Color Tool

The Color tool resembles a bucket of paint. (Try not to let the practical joker in you run wild with possibilities.) You use the Color tool to alter event colors. However, you must first determine which color to use by clicking the Select Colors menu located to the right of the Color tool shown in Figure 1.21.

Figure 1.21: Location of the Color Select menu

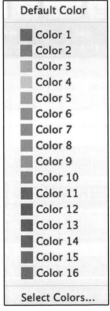

Figure 1.22: Color list

When you click on the Color Select menu, a list of sixteen selectable colors will appear, as shown in Figure 1.22. If you're really into specific colors or you are colorblind and wish to define your own colors, you can choose Select Colors from the bottom of the menu to open a palette of colors from which to choose or design.

After you've selected a color, you can paint the event by clicking on it.

Other Color Tool Procedures

You can use the Object Selection tool or a Select All command and Shift-click the selected events to change all of their colors. Ctrl/Command-clicking an event will reveal a small, horizontal color palette with which you can select a different color. This method is very useful for changing the color of many events with different colors. Alt/Option-clicking an event will assign its color to the Color tool.

The Status, Info, and Overview Lines

The Status, Info, and Overview Lines can be very useful during the editing process. However, they're not always visible. Clicking on the Window Layout button located at the upper left-hand corner of the Project window shown in Figure 1.23 will allow you to make each of the lines visible.

When the Window Layout settings are visible, a blue, opaque mask will cover the rest of the Project window. That mask indicates there's another window open. This is a common behavior in Cubase. To close the window, simply click anywhere on the blue mask, or if you wait a few seconds, it will close automatically. However, whether you close it or it closes automatically, make sure to put checks next to the Status Line, Info Line, and Overview boxes.

The Location of the Lines

Each of the lines is located directly underneath the Toolbar, as seen in Figure 1.24.

Figure 1.23: The Window Layout settings

Figure 1.24: The Status, Info, and Overview Lines

The Status Line

The Status Line displays the current settings in the Project Setup window, which can be revealed by clicking the Project menu and selecting Project Setup, or by typing Shift + S. You can also click on the Status Line to reveal the Project Setup settings. The Status Line itself displays four fields: Record Time Max, Record Format, Project Frame Rate, and Project Pan Law. However, there are many more settings in the Project Setup window, the most significant of which I'll go over in a moment.

All but Record Time Max are configured in the Project Setup window. Instead, Record Time Max keeps a running tally of how much recording can be performed on the drive where the Project (and Project Folder) is stored. This is especially useful to monitor when you're recording audio projects with lots of tracks, or when you've done so much recording that your hard disk is filling up. (Lucky you!) If you want to hide the Status Line but still monitor the record time, there's a larger Record Time Max window located under the Devices menu.

The Project Setup Window

It's best to configure these settings before you do any recording. That's because making changes afterward can be very problematic. For example, if you've recorded audio files at 48.000 kHz and then change the Project Settings to a sample rate of 44.100 kHz, the speed and pitch of the 48 kHz files will be altered during playback. That's why it's critical to set them right the first time. I would recommend that unless you have the specific need to do otherwise, you configure your Project Setup window as it is in Figure 1.25.

The most common sample frequency for musicians using DAW programs is 44.100 kHz. That's because audio CDs and consumer-friendly MP3 files are 44.100 kHz. However, if you're working on audio for film or video, you'll want to set the sample rate to 48.000 kHz. If you are working on projects you know will be converted to other DAW programs that are incapable of deciphering 32-bit files (such as Pro Tools 9 or earlier), you should set the bit resolution to 24-bit. Most modern DAW programs can read 24-bit files, so only in the rarest of circumstances would you need to choose 16-bit.

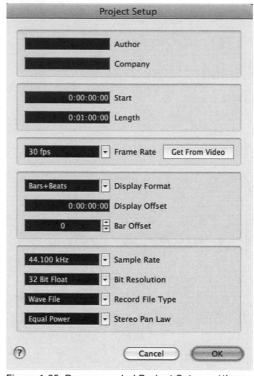

Figure 1.25: Recommended Project Setup settings

If want to avail yourself of the high-resolution sample rate capability of your audio interface (i.e., higher than 48.000 kHz), I would recommend 88.200 kHz for music projects and 96.000 kHz for video projects. However, most high-resolution disciples choose 96.000 kHz, 192.000 kHz, or even 384.000 kHz, regardless of the destination medium of the final product. But bear in mind that the sample rates of current consumer audio products max out at 48.000 kHz. Therefore, your end listener will not be able to fully enjoy the sonic advantages of high-resolution sample rates. Recording in high resolution is mainly for your benefit, but can be important for "future proofing" your music if compatible consumer products are introduced at a future date.

The Info Line

The Info Line displays very detailed information on one or more selected events. The data that appears in the Info Line will differ somewhat depending on what type of event is selected. For example, Figure 1.26 shows the Info Line values for a single MIDI event.

Figure 1.26: Info Line values for a MIDI event

For now, let's concentrate on the Info Line as it pertains to MIDI and Audio events.

Info Line Data Common to MIDI and Audio Events
- Start: Start location of the event.
- End: End location of the event.
- Length: Overall length of the event.
- Offset: Timing offset of the data within the event.
- Mute: Mute condition of the event. (See Mute tool.)
- Lock: Indicates if an event is locked out of editing.
- Transpose: The value to which the event is being transposed.
- Global Transpose: Whether the event follows the Transpose track or not.
- Root Key: Establishes the root key of the event.

Info Line Data for MIDI Events
- Name: The name of the event.
- Velocity: The positive or negative velocity offset.

Info Line Data for Audio Events
- File: The name of the Audio file depicted by the event.
- Description: The name of the event.
- Volume: The volume of the event in dB (decibels).
- Fine-Tune: Tuning values finer than a semitone.

Editing the Info Line Values
Editing values on the Info Line is accomplished by a variety of methods. If the data is alphanumeric (such as Name or Description), you can double-click the current value and use your computer keyboard to enter the desired value. For timing data (such as Start and Length), you can employ the double-click method, or you can click and drag to increase or decrease the value. For finer control, you can hover the mouse over the value. Hovering slightly above the horizontal midline of the value will add a small "+" icon to the mouse, and clicking will increment the value. Similarly, hovering below the horizontal midline of the value will reveal a small "-" icon to the mouse, and clicking will decrement the value. Strictly numeric values (such as Volume and Fine-Tune) can be double-clicked, or Alt/Option-clicking will reveal a vertical value slider you can adjust up or down. Data that have predetermined values (such as Global Transpose or Mute) can be edited by clicking the data, which will reveal a list or switch between two different values.

Editing Multiple Selected Events
By using the Object Selection tool to select multiple events, you can edit the values of all the selected events. When a single event is selected, the alphanumeric values in the Info Line are a light blue. When multiple events are selected, the values turn orange. When you edit timing values, the selected events will retain their positions relative to one another. However, you can hold Ctrl/Command while editing the timing values to adjust all the events identically. This is useful for selecting several events at varying locations and placing them all at a specific location.

The Overview Line
The Overview Line is simply a very small depiction of the events in the Event Display. It is useful for monitoring your current position, especially on lengthy projects. It also offers some very useful zooming capabilities that we'll discuss in a moment. (See "Zooming with the Overview Line.") The Overview Line depicts both events and the visible region of the Event Display, as seen in Figure 1.27.

Figure 1.27: The Overview Line and Event Display

I had to dramatically resize the Event Display to illustrate how the Overview works. As you can see, it displays all events, whether they're currently visible in the Event Display or not. But it also depicts the entire length of the project at all times. If you notice that there's a bit of void area on the right side of the Overview Line, you'll want to adjust the Length setting in the Project Setup window (see Figure 1.25) to accurately depict the overall length of the project. However, if you start recording past the project Length setting, it will be lengthened automatically.

Zooming Techniques and the Event Display

Zooming refers to how much data you can currently see. Think of a camera with a zoom lens. A wide zoom reveals a broader spectrum but less detail. A tight zoom reveals a smaller spectrum but more detail. In the same way, you can alter both the vertical and horizontal zoom settings of many windows, including the Event Display. Therefore, many of the techniques I will discuss in this section are applicable to the Key Editor, Sample Editor, and many other windows. Changing the zoom allows you to customize the display to make the process of editing easier.

Horizontal Zoom

While there are more conventional methods, I'm going to show you my favorite zoom technique first. Once you start using it, you'll wish every temporally based software program (DAW programs, nonlinear video editors, scientific programs, etc.) would use this zoom technique. I call it the "drag" zoom. Click and hold your mouse on the Time Ruler at the top of the Event Display, then drag up to zoom out or down to zoom in. Figure 1.28 further demonstrates this powerful zoom method.

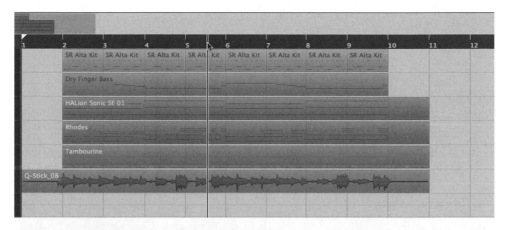

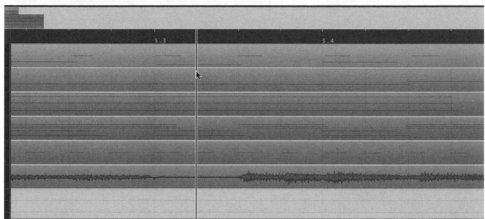

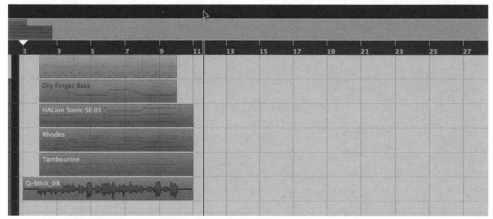

Figure 1.28: Drag zooming

Holding the Shift key while drag zooming will lock the cursor position. This is useful for maintaining the focus of your zoom without accidentally moving the cursor to the left or right.

There are also key commands for zooming: "G" to zoom out and "H" to zoom in. And if you're really into convention, there are Zoom sliders in the lower right-hand corner of the Event Display, as shown in Figure 1.29.

Zooming with the Overview Line

When you move your mouse into the Overview Line, it will resemble a pencil. That allows you to click and drag a range inside of the Overview Line to define a zoom. The

Figure 1.29: The Zoom sliders

zoom will appear as a slightly dark box around the range you drew. Then if you hover over that range, the mouse becomes a hand, allowing you to drag the entire zoom range from left to right. Or if you hover near the left or right boundary of the zoom range, the mouse becomes left and right arrows, allowing you to stretch or shrink the zoom range.

Vertical Zoom

When you zoom vertically in the Event Display, you're essentially making the track heights taller or shorter. Locate the Vertical Zoom slider in Figure 1.29, and adjust it up and down. Both the events and the height of the tracks they reside on will become taller or shorter, as shown in Figure 1.30.

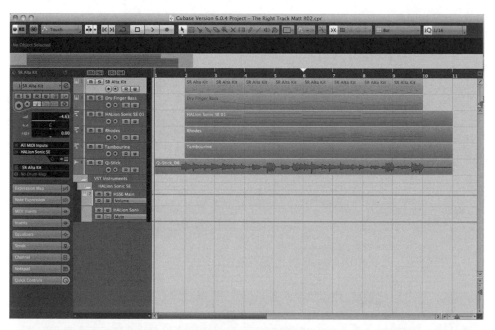

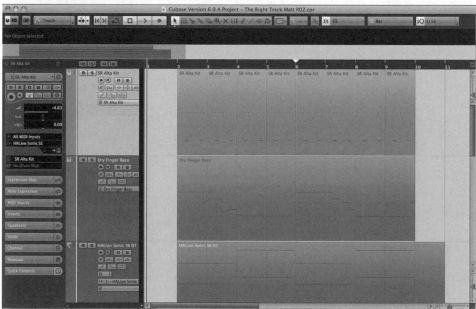

Figure 1.30: Adjusting the Vertical Zoom slider

Zooming Track Heights

When adjusting the Vertical Zoom slider, it will adjust the track height of all tracks equally. Another method is to use the Zoom tool while holding Ctrl/Command. You can also adjust the vertical zoom on a track-by-track basis by adjusting the track heights. Simply hover over the top or bottom boundary of a track in the track column, as shown in Figure 1.31.

Figure 1.31: Track height adjustment, track by track

The mouse will appear as two small, parallel lines with arrows at the top and bottom. Clicking and dragging up and down will adjust the height of the track. Holding Ctrl/Command, then clicking to drag will adjust all track heights simultaneously. You can also select multiple tracks (the tracks, not their associated events) and adjust all their heights by adjusting only one selected track.

Zoom Commands and Their Key Commands

The Zoom commands are a great way to adjust the gross zoom of the Event Display. Click on the Edit menu, select the Zoom category, and select a command from the list that appears in Figure 1.32.

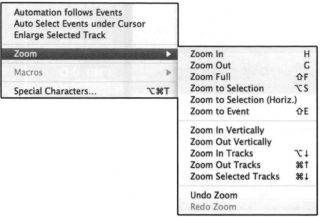

Figure 1.32: The Edit menu Zoom commands

The commands are self-explanatory. You'll also notice that many of the commands have key commands assigned to them. A few of my favorites are Alt/Option + E to zoom one selected event, Alt/Option + S to zoom more than one selected event, and Shift + F to display all of the events horizontally.

Additional Zoom Commands

There are additional Zoom command menus located near the vertical and horizontal sliders shown in Figure 1.33.

Clicking on the Zoom menus will reveal the associated Zoom commands shown in Figure 1.34.

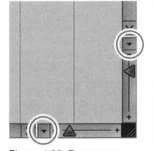

Figure 1.33: Zoom commands by the Zoom sliders

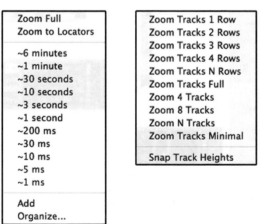

Figure 1.34: Horizontal and Vertical Zoom menu commands

The horizontal commands are time based, allowing you to zoom to specific time ranges. The vertical commands are based on the number of tracks you'd like displayed. My favorite command is Zoom N Tracks. After selecting it, a dialog box will appear, allowing you to type in a numeric value. This is very useful when you have multiple associated tracks. For example, if you have 10 drum tracks you'd like visible for editing, enter a value of 10, and all the track heights will be zoomed to view 10 tracks at a time.

Event Zoom

The Event Zoom slider is located at the upper left-hand corner of the Event Display. Its location and function are shown in Figure 1.35.

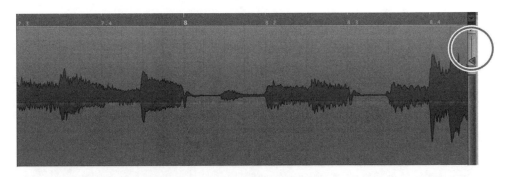

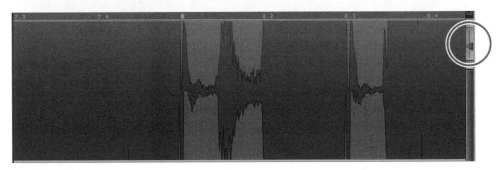

Figure 1.35: Event Zoom slider

The Event Zoom only affects Audio events. But as you can see, the audio waveform contained within an Audio event will become magnified. This will allow you to see quiet passages more easily, and therefore, editing will become easier.

A common misconception of the Event Slider is that it affects the volume of the audio data. This is not the case. Even though the data looks like it's getting louder, only visual representation of the audio data is being affected.

Advanced Behaviors of the Event Display

Before we can start editing our events, we'll need to understand how Cubase handles events when they overlap. That overlapping concept is also critical for understanding a powerful new feature that first appeared in Cubase 6: Comping. So significant is Comping that we'll need a separate chapter to discuss it in. We'll do that next.

Chapter **2**

COMPING AND OVERLAPPING EVENTS

At this point, I hope you've been doing a lot of recording and that you've been using MIDI, Instrument, and Audio tracks. You should also be familiar with how MIDI events and Audio events differ from one another. But it's easy to get the behaviors of MIDI and Audio events confused. Since MIDI is used on both MIDI and Instrument tracks, their events are interchangeable. However, MIDI events cannot be placed on Audio tracks, and vice versa. In fact, most of the thirteen track types that Cubase uses contain specific noninterchangeable events. We'll cover most of those other tracks in chapter 5. But until then, we need to learn about overlapping events and a wonderful creative Cubase function known as *Comping*. In this chapter, you will learn:

- MIDI events *can* overlap.
- Audio events should *not* overlap.
- The basics of Comping.
- How to reveal and edit the Comping Lanes.

Understanding Event Overlaps

When you start editing the events in the Event Display, it's very easy to move, delete, copy, and rearrange the events. However, it's critical to understand how only certain events can be moved to specific track types. To illustrate this, we'll be using a project from the disc that comes with this book. It's located in the Cubase Projects Folder, and the folder name is "Overlaps." (See appendix A, "Using the Included Disc.") Inside that folder, load the project "Overlaps R01.cpr."

Exploring the "Overlaps R01" Project

The "Overlaps R01" project contains three Instrument tracks and two Audio tracks and should appear similarly to Figure 2.1.

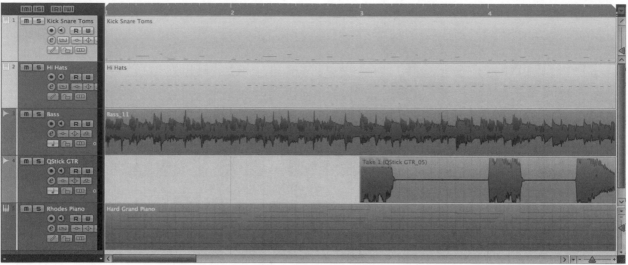

Figure 2.1: The Track Column and Event Display of the "Overlaps R01" project

The project was created in Cubase 6, so it's possible that if you're using Cubase 6 Artist or a lower version, the Instrument tracks may not contain the same sounds. If that's the case, go ahead and assign different yet similar sounds to the Instrument tracks. In other words, tracks 1 and 2 are drum sets, and track 5 is an electric piano. Then start playback, and have a listen to all the tracks. The cycle mode is on, so the same four measures will repeat over and over until you stop playback. While it's playing, solo each track so that you get an idea of the sounds contained within the events. Also notice that when you hover your mouse over any of the events, it will darken slightly and its event handles will become visible.

Identifying Event Overlaps

When your mouse hovers over overlapping events, their appearance is quite different. Instead of only a slightly darker background, you'll see vertical pinstripes running across the events. For example, with your Object Selection tool, drag the Hi Hats event over the Kick Snare Toms event. You can do this whether Cubase is playing or not. But if you are in Playback mode while you do this, you'll notice that the characteristics of the Hi Hats sounds will be slightly different. That's because the Hi Hats track has a different instrument assigned to it than does the Kick Snare Toms track. However, the MIDI notes for the Hi Hats are identical to both tracks, which is why you'll still hear the Hi Hats sounds. But the most significant thing to realize is that you can still hear *both* events. When MIDI events overlap, they'll both be audible. Now when you hover your mouse over the events on track 1, they appear with the vertical pinstripes that indicate an overlap, as shown in Figure 2.2.

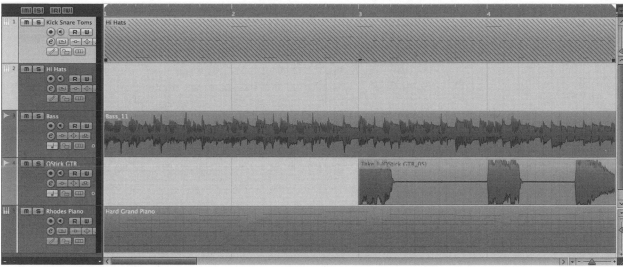

Figure 2.2: Overlapping events

Since both events had identical start and end times, the pinstripes will appear across the entire range of the overlap. However, if you were to adjust the handle of the Hi Hats event, you will see how the overlap range follows the topmost event, as shown in Figure 2.3.

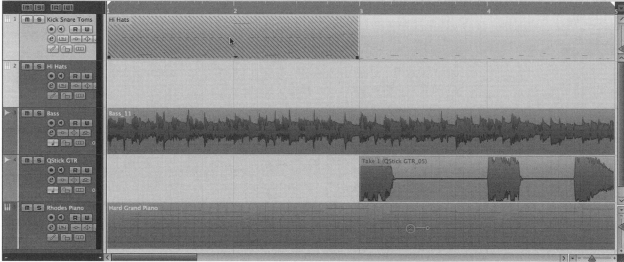

Figure 2.3: Overlap range after event resize

Now type Ctrl/Command + Z (Undo) to return the Hi Hats event to its original size. (See Figure 2.2.)

Overlapping MIDI Events

You've already discovered how overlapping MIDI events can coexist on the same track. This offers both creative freedoms and creative conundrums. The ability to layer multiple MIDI events can create very dense results. But then the editing gets a little foreboding. For example, the Object Selection tool will always select the topmost event. When using the Split, Erase, Mute, or Play tools, only the topmost event will be edited. However, when using the Range Selection tool, all of the events (even several layers deep) get selected. Try some of these edits on the Hi Hats event, and see how and if the Kick Snare Toms event is affected. After you've tried a few edits, undo to the point where you first opened the project. (See Figure 2.1.)

When Overlapping MIDI Won't Work

When you were listening to the overlapping Hi Hats and Kick Snare Toms events, the audible difference was in what type of hi hat sound was being produced. As I mentioned before, this is because the MIDI notes were identical between the instruments loaded on tracks 1 and 2. But what if you overlapped MIDI events that had very different track sounds? To find out, with the Object Selection tool, click and drag the Rhodes Piano event on top of the Hi Hats event. Release the mouse button, and start playback (if you haven't already done so). Notice how the sound of the piano goes away but has been replaced with some cymbal and percussion sounds. This is the result of incompatible MIDI performances. Basically, the lesson to be learned is that the sound comes from the instrument assigned to the track, not from the event itself.

For a more dramatic example of this concept, drag the Kick Snare Toms event to the now-empty Rhodes Piano track. Solo the Rhodes track and listen to the results. If you're like me, you'll hear music that might accompany silly cartoon characters as they march down the street. But whatever you see in your mind's eye, you certainly won't be hearing drums. Now that you know you can overlap multiple MIDI events, remember that the track rather than the event determines the sound used for playback.

Overlapping Audio Events

The behavior of overlapping Audio events is much different than that of MIDI events. For example, the Overlaps Project has two Audio tracks: Bass and Q-Stick GTR. The "Bass_11" event plays throughout the entire four measures; however, the "Q-Stick GTR_05" event plays for only the last two measures. With the Object Selection tool, click and drag the "Q-Stick GTR_05" event over the top of the "Bass_11," and release the mouse button. When you listen to the playback, you'll notice that the "Q-Stick GTR_05" event cancels out the "Bass_11" event underneath. That's because as opposed to MIDI, only one overlapping Audio event can be played on a track. That event will be the topmost event, and events underneath that will not be heard.

Handling Audio Event Overlaps

You might conclude that since Audio events cannot be layered like MIDI events, you'll need to be thriftier with the number of Audio events you add to or record into a project. This is not true. Cubase (the full version) has unlimited Audio tracks; you can simply place those events onto their own tracks. Lower versions of Cubase will have finite track counts. (Cubase Artist has sixty-four Audio tracks; Cubase Elements, forty-eight; Cubase AI, thirty-two; and Cubase LE, sixteen.) When you consider that many Beatles recordings were made on 4-track recorders, even entry-level Cubase versions will provide you with a lot of Audio-event overlapping capabilities.

There is one situation in which Audio events can overlap, albeit for brief moments. That can occur when joining two Audio events adjacently on the same track(s). In this case, it's very common to use a crossfade to smooth the transition between the end of one event and the start of another. We'll explore crossfades in chapter 4, "Editing Audio Data."

Using the "Move to" Commands

After comprehending the limitations of over-lapping Audio events, most people try to avoid them. However, there are situations, especially with MIDI events, where overlapping can offer some creative possibilities. For this reason, Cubase has ways of arranging the overlapping events. These are the Move to commands, and they're located under the Edit menu, as shown in Figure 2.4.

Using the Move to commands to rearrange the layers of events on a track: Move to Front will bring the selected layer to the surface of the track and can be invoked by typing the "U" key on your computer keyboard. Move to Back will submerge the selected event to the bottom of the track.

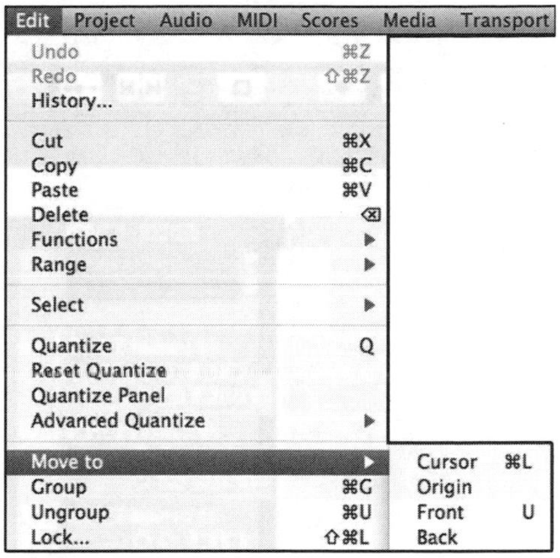

Merging Overlaps with the Glue Tool

In chapter 1, we learned how the Glue tool can merge adjacent events together into a larger single event. In a similar way, the Glue tool can merge overlapped events into a single event. If you glue Audio events together, their playback priority (topmost always audible) is maintained and will therefore be heard with their preglued priority. (Audio events glued in this way can be unglued later using the Dissolve Part command on the Audio menu.) Basically, gluing the overlapping events can make it much easier to move or otherwise edit a series of events.

Figure 2.4: The Move to Front and Move to Back commands

But with MIDI events, the Glue tool will combine all of the MIDI data from the overlapping events into a single event. For example, with the Object Selection tool, click and drag the Hi Hats event over the Kick Snare Toms event. (See Figure 2.2.) Then select the Glue tool and click the Hi Hats event to merge the contents of both events into one single event. The event will retain the name of the topmost event—in this case, the event is named "Hi Hats."

There might also come a time when you want to glue all the events of a single track together. Right/Ctrl-click on the track (in the Track column), and choose Select All Events from the minimenu. Then select the Glue tool and Shift-click on any selected event. All of the overlapping events, regardless of how many layers deep, will be glued together as one contiguous event.

Comping

Cubase 6 was the first version to introduce users to an amazing new feature called Comping. It uses the unlimited Audio track playback capability of Cubase to composite several good takes into one great take. But before we can fully understand the power of Comping, we need to understand how the need for it developed.

A Brief History of Multitrack Audio Compositing

In the days of analog recording, track counts usually ranged from two to twenty-four. While it was possible to synchronize multiple analog tape machines together to increase track counts, the cost of both equipment and tape stock was prohibitive to all but the big-name bands. So with only sixteen or twenty-four tracks, we still had to strive for the best "take." That is, recording a performer over and over again until we captured the best performance. Every time we recorded a new take, the previous take was erased. Or in the rare case of leftover empty tracks, we could record multiple takes and later choose which ones to keep. Either way, the limits of technology forced us to "keep the best and punch the rest." That is to say, keep the best take and use the technique of punch in/out recording to fix any remaining flubs on that take.

When digital recorders and DAW software entered the recording studio, track counts increased dramatically. Today with Cubase, the only limitation to track counts is the power of your computer. Modern computers can easily play back a lot of tracks, as shown in Figure 2.5.

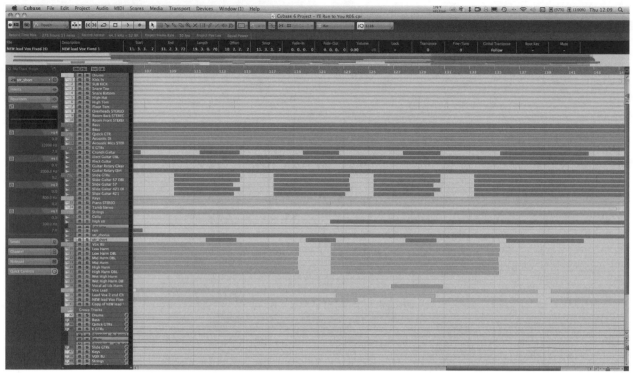

Figure 2.5: A mid-sized 41-Audio track project running on a MacBook Pro

Higher track counts allowed us to record multiple takes onto multiple tracks and edit them to create the best take. This technique is known as *compositing* and is still used in many contemporary DAW programs.

Cubase Introduces Comping

When the developers at Steinberg took a close look at how Cubase users were using multiple compositing tracks, they realized there was a golden opportunity to make the process more elegant. This process is known as Comping. Instead of making users record onto multiple tracks, they added Comping "lanes" to every track, and every recording take is placed on the same track but in its own lane. Therefore, all of the takes exist on one track, rather than spanning across several tracks. Then, by editing the events on each lane, you can assemble the best event from multiple takes. So the results of Comping are identical to compositing. However, as you'll see, the Comping editing process is much easier.

Recording Audio Tracks for Comping

Before Comping, I would usually record a take, and if I thought I wouldn't use it, I would stop, hit Undo, and record a new take. But with Comping, unless the current recording is an obvious disaster, I'll keep every take. That means you're going to end up with a lot of overlapping Audio events. But as you already know, only the most recently recorded take will be audible, because it will be the topmost event.

Figure 2.6: Audio Record Mode setting

Before you start recording your Audio tracks, you must make sure that Cubase will keep every take. Look at the far left of the Transport Panel, and take note of the current Audio Record Mode, as seen in Figure 2.6.

If the mode is Keep History, you're all set. Keep History is the default setting, so unless you've changed modes, you shouldn't have to change it back. But if you do, click on the current setting to reveal the Audio

Record Mode setting, and choose Keep History. Now every time you create new audio recordings on an Audio track, Cubase will keep every take.

Revealing the Comping Lanes

For the rest of this chapter, I would recommend loading the "Comping R01.cpr" project from the disc included with this book. (See appendix A, "Using the Included Disc.") That way, you can follow along with the examples, and you won't put one of your own projects at risk.

When you've recorded several takes on an Audio track, it will appear as if you've only recorded once. That's because all the takes are overlapping on the track, as seen in Figure 2.7.

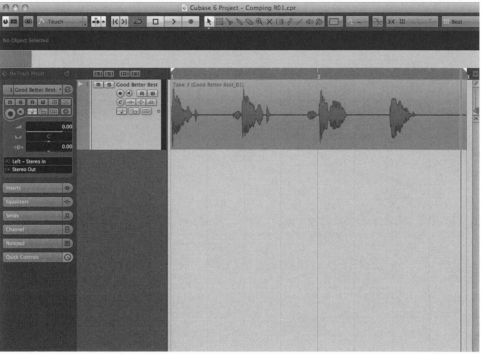

Figure 2.7: Several overlapping Audio events

To reveal the Comping lanes, you'll need to click the Show Lanes button on the track. However, depending on the current track height, you might not be able to see the button. Increase the track height (see chapter 1, Figure 1.31) to reveal the Show Lanes button, as shown in Figure 2.7. When you click on the Show Lanes button, the Comping Lanes will drop down below the track, as shown in Figure 2.8.

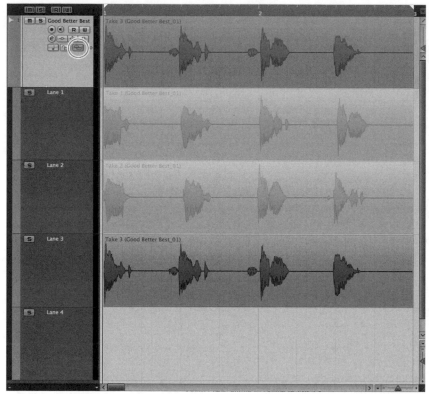

Figure 2.8: The Comping Lanes and Show Lanes button

At first glance, you might presume that you're looking at a bunch of Audio tracks. However, instead of by the track number and name, the lanes are identified by a number (Lane 1, Lane 2, etc.). The number of visible lanes will depend on how many takes have been recorded on the source track and will match the track color. The last take is currently audible and appears normally, while the previous takes are inaudible and slightly dimmer in appearance.

Auditioning and Choosing Takes

Confirm that the project has Cycle enabled on the Transport Panel, then start playback and listen to take 3. It should say, "Best, Best, Better, Good." (You'll see how we're going to use the words contained within these takes in a moment.) During the cycling playback, use the Object Selection tool, and click on any event in a Comping Lane to make it audible. Doing so will mute out the previously selected take. For example, click on take 2, and you'll hear, "Good, Good, Better, Best." Click on take 1, and you'll hear, "Good, Good, Best, Better." If one of the takes has the best overall performance, you can leave it selected and close the lanes by clicking the Show Lanes button shown in Figure 2.8.

However, it's more likely that you'll need to edit the events in the lanes to get the best possible performance. You'll notice that among all of the takes you've auditioned so far, none of them says, "Best, Best, Best, Best." In other words, every take contains at least one "Good" and "Better" along with the "Bests." Since the goal of compositing and Comping is to get the "best" performance possible, we'll need to edit the events in the lanes to get the "Best, Best, Best, Best" result. (Now you understand why these events say what they say.)

Editing the Takes Within the Comping Lanes

The goal of this exercise is to get all the takes on the Comping lanes to say, "Best, Best, Best, Best." With that in mind, listen to take 3. It contains the most "Bests," so leave it selected. I did this on purpose, because it's very common to get the best recording on the latest take. But toward the end of take 3, the performance degrades, represented by the "Better" and "Good." Let's see if there are some "Bests" on the other takes.

Editing Comping Events by Resizing

For this type of editing to work, verify that Snap is disabled. (See Figure 2.7.) Then, with the Object Selection tool in Normal Sizing mode, click and drag the right handle of the third take, as shown in Figure 2.9.

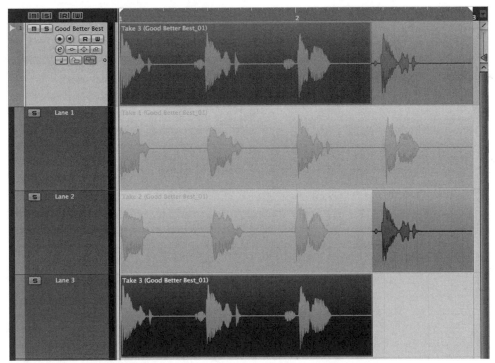

Figure 2.9: Resizing take 3

When you resize a take, the event from the preceding Comping Lane will become audible. Now during playback, you'll hear "Best, Best, Better" from take 3 and "Best" from take 2. So by resizing take 3, we end up with, "Best, Best, Better, Best." But if you're like me, you want the best possible result. So perhaps take 2 has a "Best" with which we can replace the "Better" on take 3. To find out, resize take 3, as shown in Figure 2.10.

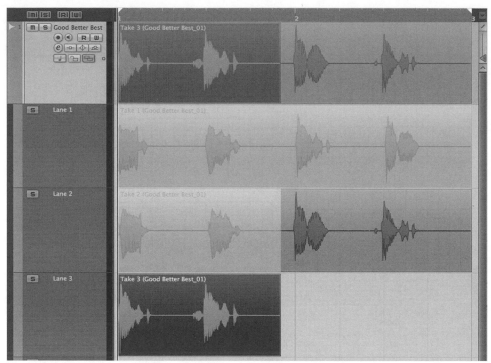

Figure 2.10: Resizing to reveal more of take 2

Unfortunately, take 2 contains another "Better" rather than a "Best." Now that we know that we won't find four "Bests" among takes 2 and 3, we'll need to look to take 1 to complete the Comping.

Editing Comping Events with the Split Tool

Click on take 1, which, dur ing playback, allows it to play in its entirety. That's because the length of the selected event will determine how much of it we hear. Since take 1 is now longer than take 3 and just as long as take 2, we only hear take 1. But in doing so, we can hear that there's a "Best" shown in Figure 2.11 that we can use to complete our edit.

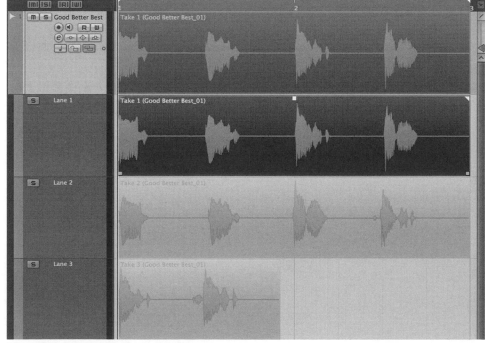

Figure 2.11: Take 1 selected and audible

Using the Split tool, click around the "Best" in take 1 to split it into three separate events, as shown in Figure 2.12.

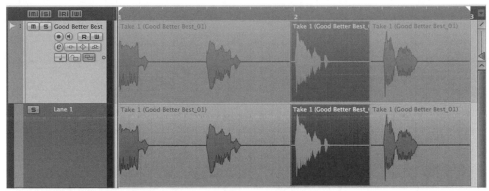

Figure 2.12: Using the Split tool on take 1

Basically, you're splitting the "Best" out of take 1. But when you listen back to the edit you just made, it will sound identical to before you split it. That's because all three events that comprise take 1 are still selected for playback. What we want to do is use the Object Selection tool to click on the events of takes 2 and 3, as shown in Figure 2.13.

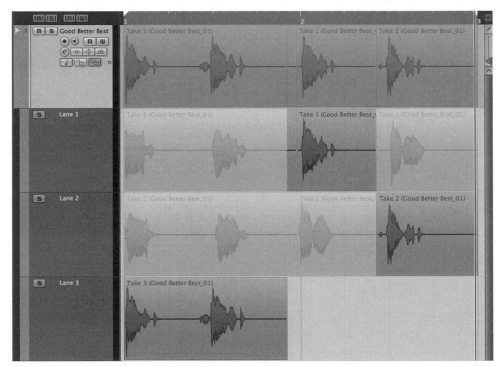

Figure 2.13: Clicking takes 2 and 3 with Object Selection tool

Now when we listen back to the result, we end up with, "Best, Best, Best, Best." So what we've ended up with is the best performance by using elements from all of the recorded takes. Since we've completed our Comping edit, we can reclaim the vertical space in the Event Display by clicking the Show Lanes button (see Figure 2.18), which will close all the Comping Lanes.

(Note: If for some reason you got lost along the way, you can load the "Comping R02.cpr" project from the disc that came with this book [see appendix A] to hear and see the completed Comping edit.)

I can't overstate how powerful the Comping feature of Cubase can be. Without it, the compositing process would require us to mute and unmute multiple tracks and use a combination of resizing and the Split and Mute tools on every single event to remove overlapping events. That would mean a lot more hassle and work for you and anyone who uses a DAW other than Cubase.

Other Comping Techniques

I've only discussed resizing the events and using the Split tool to edit the Comping events. However, you can also use the Range Selection, Glue, Erase, and Mute tools to further refine your Comping session. You can even use the Object Selection tool to click and drag events from different times and even different takes or tracks to make the best possible Comping edit.

But by far my favorite tool to use during Comping edits is the Play tool. With it, you can click on any event, whether it's currently selected for playback or not, to audition the audio data within the event. For example, when we were looking for the last "Best" to complete our edit, I could have used the Play tool and clicked on take 1 to audibly search for possibilities.

It's also important to realize that all of the edits you make during a Comping session are nondestructive. Therefore, you can split, resize, mute, and even erase to your heart's content without risk of losing any of your takes. We'll explore more of this nondestructive editing concept later, especially when we start editing audio data in chapter 4. But now, in chapter 3, let's learn about editing MIDI data.

Chapter 3

EDITING MIDI AND INSTRUMENT DATA

When the MIDI Specification was released in the early 1980s, it brought musicians unprecedented control and editing possibilities. Not only could MIDI data be recorded and played back like audio recordings, but it could also be edited with microscopic precision. Individual notes within a chord could be manipulated or edited without disturbing the other notes around them. And since MIDI consisted of more than just note data, elements such as pitch bend, sustain pedal, and volume controllers could be edited with remarkable accuracy.

(Note: Before reading this chapter, you should be aware that a large part of the editing process is making proper selections. Therefore, it will be very important to have read chapter 1 before proceeding further.)

For almost thirty years, very little has changed about MIDI. However, the methods for editing MIDI data have become very refined. And when MIDI-controlled, computer-based virtual instruments hit the scene in the late 1990s, many musicians, producers, and music enthusiasts indoctrinated themselves into the MIDI world. In this chapter, we'll be looking at the many ways to edit MIDI in Cubase, including:

- The relationship MIDI shares with MIDI and Instrument tracks.
- The components of MIDI data.
- Editing MIDI events in the Event Display.
- Editing MIDI data in the Key Editor and In-Place Editor.
- Exploring the MIDI Functions and Logical Presets.

MIDI Data in Cubase

There are two Cubase track types upon which you can record MIDI data: MIDI tracks and Instrument tracks. The ways in which the MIDI data is recorded, manipulated, and edited on the tracks are identical. The only difference is the ultimate destination for that MIDI data. MIDI tracks can send data to VST (virtual) Instruments in Cubase or to external MIDI devices via a MIDI interface. However, Instrument tracks can only send data to the VST Instruments to which they're assigned. But due to Cubase's flexibility, the events on MIDI and Instrument tracks can be freely exchanged or shared.

A Brief MIDI Primer

Over the years, the applications and advantages of MIDI recording have been wildly misunderstood. I still hear people say things such as, "MIDI is inferior to audio" and "MIDI sounds bad." Statements like those are usually perpetuated by users who don't understand what MIDI is and how to use it. By now you should realize that MIDI data is not sound and that both audio and MIDI recordings have their own distinct advantages and disadvantages. So instead of going over all types of MIDI data at length, let's learn about the most common MIDI data you'll be using in Cubase. (Note: For a thorough description of MIDI, I recommend *The MIDI Companion Book* from Hal Leonard.)

MIDI Note Data

Throughout the rest of this book, I'll be discussing MIDI real-time data. That is to say, the data used when recording musical passages from a MIDI controller (such as a keyboard or drum pad controller). MIDI is not sound; rather, it is a series of actions. Those actions are representations of how the performer manipulates the musical instrument when he or she is playing it. For example, the most commonly recorded MIDI data is note on/off data. When a performer plays middle C on a MIDI controller (note on) that is then recorded on a MIDI track, Cubase captures the MIDI note number (pitch), how hard it was played (velocity), and when the note is released (note off).

MIDI Continuous Controllers

If MIDI could only represent note data, it couldn't depict the entire musical performance. For example, what happens when a pianist steps down on the sustain or other pedals? Plus, not all instruments generate notes the same way. When you press down notes on a piano, the piano will generate an audible sound. But when you press down notes on a violin, nothing happens. Audible sound is only generated when a bow is pushed across the violin strings. How are those actions represented in the MIDI Specification?

The developers of MIDI realized that they needed a specification that could depict all of the actions a musician could perform upon a real musical instrument. To that end, MIDI control numbers (known as continuous controllers, controllers, or CCs) were added to the spec. For example, when the sustain pedal attached to a MIDI keyboard is pressed, MIDI controller 4 is sent with a value of 127 (on). When the pedal is released, MIDI controller 4 is sent again, but this time with a value of 0 (off). Similarly, MIDI controller 11 is used to represent expression and can be used to represent the volume of notes being generated on a violin. MIDI controller 11 has a continuous range, as many controllers do, from 0 to 127. (Some hardware and software manufacturers represent MIDI controller values in a range of 1 to 128, which can result in numeric inconsistencies.)

Other Commonly Used MIDI Data Types

While not an actual MIDI continuous controller, pitch bend is very common. Pitch bend is usually generated by the pitch bend wheel found on many MIDI keyboards, and can simulate the pitch effects created by musical instruments such as violins, woodwinds, and guitars. Similar to MIDI pitch bend, some keyboards can also transmit aftertouch, which is how much pressure is applied to a MIDI note while it's being played.

MIDI program changes are used to automate the selection of sounds within a synthesizer. Originally, MIDI had 128 program change numbers. That was more than enough, because early MIDI devices only had thirty-two or forty onboard sounds. However, as technology progressed, it became possible for MIDI-compatible synthesizer manufacturers to install thousands of sounds inside of one device. How do you get to those sounds with only 128 program changes? Well, the MIDI specification was modified to include a new data type known as bank select messages. They are MIDI continuous controllers

00 (MSB, Most Significant Byte) and 32 (LSB, or Least Significant Byte) and are used to determine which sound bank a MIDI program change will reference. For example, if you want to call up a synthesizer's eleventh sound located in the fourth internal sound bank, a 00 bank select message of value 4 followed by a program change of 11 might be the right combination. But since every manufacturer implements bank select messages differently, you'll need to consult the owner's manual or MIDI implementation chart to determine how to use them.

MIDI Editing in the Event Display

Many of the most common MIDI edits, such as quantizing and transposing, can be performed in the Event Display. The advantage is that the edits are applied to all the data in the event, or multiple events across multiple tracks. So bear in mind that when you edit a MIDI or Instrument event in the Event Display, you're editing the MIDI data contained within that event.

It's also important to know that the types of editing you're going to learn about can be accomplished in a number of ways. I'll try to cover the most basic methods, but be aware that, as with most things in Cubase, there's more than one way to perform an edit. For the first part of this chapter, I would recommend loading "The Right Track R03.cpr" project from the disc that comes with this book. (See appendix A, "Using the Included Disc.")

Quantizing MIDI Events

Quantizing is a fancy word for the auto-correction of timing. It also happens to be the most overused MIDI edit, and I'll explain why in a moment. But for now, let's quantize some events in the Event Display. Mute the Q-Stick track, and start playback to audition the MIDI and Instrument tracks. You can hear that the timing of the recordings are a little loose and could be improved by quantization. We'll start with the Bass track, so go ahead and solo the Dry Finger Bass track, and listen to the playback. Since this track contains only single events rather than chords, it will be easier to hear the results of the quantize. Using the Object Selection tool, click on the Dry Finger Bass event and then select the Quantize Preset of 1/16, as shown in Figure 3.1.

1/16 Quantize Preset
selected

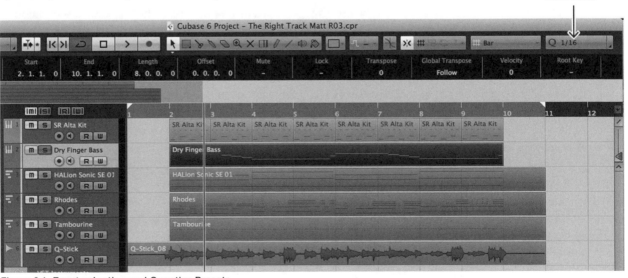

Figure 3.1: Event selection and Quantize Presets

Notice also in Figure 3.1 that the iQ setting is disabled. We'll go over iQ in a moment, but for now, make sure it's set to Q rather than iQ. The Quantize Preset of 1/16 means that the MIDI notes on the selected events will be pushed or pulled to the nearest 16th note. Since the shortest note played on the Dry Finger Bass event is an eighth note, a 16th-note preset should work well. Choosing the appropriate Quantize Preset is critical but can also really mess up the timing, depending on how loosely the original recording was performed. Rest assured that Cubase can remove the quantization applied to MIDI events or data at any time to restore the original performance.

To execute the quantize, click on the Edit menu and select Quantize, or just type "Q" on your computer keyboard. You can leave the playback engaged to instantly audition the results of the quantize. When you listen to the quantized event, you'll notice that the timing is perfect. (But perfect timing usually creates a musically boring result. More on that in a moment.) What you've just performed is known as a hard quantize. That is, the notes have been pushed or pulled to perfect 16th-note precision.

Quantizing Multiple MIDI Events on Multiple Tracks

You might find yourself needing to quantize a whole bunch of MIDI events. In that case, all you need to do is make the proper selection of events. For example, in Figure 3.2, holding Shift and clicking on each one with the Object Selection tool has selected three events.

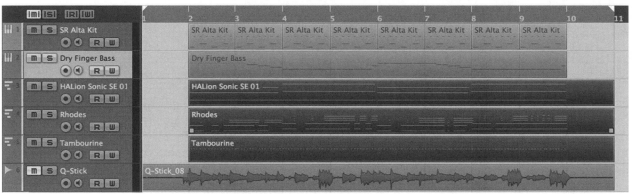

Figure 3.2: Three events selected for editing

Since you've already selected an appropriate Quantize Preset (1/16), you can execute the quantize as you did before. (My preferred method is typing the "Q" key on the computer keyboard.) Now all three events have their MIDI notes placed perfectly on the nearest 16th note.

Quantizing Multiple MIDI Events on a Single Track

The Drum track in this project has eight events placed back to back. If you want to quantize specific events, all you have to do is select them first. However, if you'd like to quantize all of the events, Right/Ctrl-click on the track, and choose Select All Events from the submenu, as shown in Figure 3.3.

Figure 3.3: The Select All Events command

The results of the Select All Events command are shown in Figure 3.4, leaving you able to execute the Quantize command.

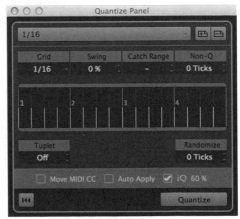

Figure 3.4: Results of the Select All Events command

Perfection Is Boring

In the same way that the Borg on *Star Trek* diminish the human experience by creating perfection, so does the hard quantize. Humans are incapable of playing perfectly in time. That's something only a computer can do. Therefore, the results of a hard quantize sterilize the human nuance right out of a musical performance and make it sound "computerized." Fortunately, resistance is not futile, and quantization is not mandatory. But Cubase does provide you with alternatives, starting with iQ.

Raising Your iQ

iQ is short for *Iterative Quantize*. iQ allows you to tighten up the timing of a MIDI recording without making the timing perfect—i.e., boring. But before we can use iQ on a track, we'll need to remove the hard quantize we've already performed. You can either type Ctrl/Command + Z several times, or select all the MIDI events and select Reset Quantize from the Edit menu. Either way, the original timing will be returned to the events. Then if you refer to Figure 3.1, you can click on the "Q" to enable iQ. Try executing a quantize with iQ enabled, and listen to the results. You should find them less computerized and more natural and human. If the timing is still too loose, you can execute another Iterative Quantize. You can even iQ as many times as you like, with each successive execution tightening the performance even more, although the end result will eventually be the same as a hard quantize. But how close to perfection will the notes be moved by the iQ? That setting is found in the Quantize Panel.

The Quantize Panel

The Quantize Panel allows you to further customize the Quantize and iQ settings and even store them as your own Quantize Presets. If you refer to Figure 3.1, you can reveal the Quantize Panel by clicking to the right of the Quantize Preset or from the Edit menu. The Quantize Panel is shown in Figure 3.5, and is a separate window that can be placed anywhere on the screen and, if desired, be left open at all times.

At the top of the Quantize Panel, you can select the Quantize Preset or use the Save/Remove buttons to save or remove your own custom presets. The Grid chooses the note value to which the Quantize command will place the notes. If your performance swings (as with swung eighth notes commonly found in jazz music), you can define the Swing percentage. Finally, the iQ Strength is located at the lower right-hand corner of the Quantize Panel. The Strength will indicate the degree to which the notes are being moved. For example, the default of 60 percent will move the notes within 60 percent of perfection. A Strength of 90 percent will move the notes even closer to perfection. I usually leave this set to 50 or 60 percent and execute multiple iQ commands until the timing feels right. But if you do want to change the Strength, you can double-click the value and type in the desired percentage,

Figure 3.5: The Quantize Panel

or you can Alt/Option-click the current percentage to reveal a vertical slider with which to adjust the Strength.

Transposing MIDI Events

Prior to MIDI, the only way to transpose a recording was to rerecord the tracks in the desired key. If you had other band members, they'd usually do so grudgingly. On the other hand, if you'd hired session musicians, they'd be elated because you'd have to once again get out your checkbook. Either way, you'd have to take the time to record the tracks all over again. But with MIDI, you can simply transpose the events.

There are many ways to transpose events, but as with quantizing (or any edit), you must first make the proper selection. (Please review the steps for quantizing multiple events earlier in this chapter for more information.) The result of transposing an event will move the MIDI note numbers higher or lower in pitch. That pitch is represented in semitones or half-steps. In other words, if you were to increase by 2 the transpose of an event containing a C major triad, the result would be a D major triad. Transposing by –2 would result in a B-flat major triad.

Transpose in the Info Line

One of the easiest ways to transpose is to adjust the Transpose value in the Info Line (see "The Status, Info, and Overview Lines" in chapter 1), as shown in Figure 3.6.

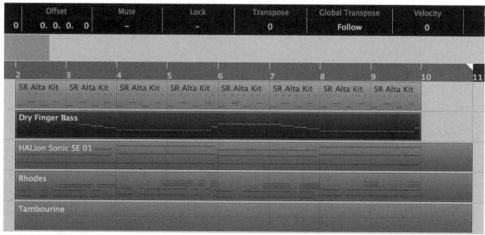

Figure 3.6: Transpose in the Info Line

Double-click on the value, and type in the number of semitones (use a negative number for downward transpositions) you'd like to move the notes within the event. Or you can Alt/Option-click on the value to reveal a vertical value slider.

You must always have at least one event selected for the Transpose value to be visible in the Info Line. If you have selected multiple events that currently have differing Transpose values, the text in the Info Line will appear in orange rather than the default light blue.

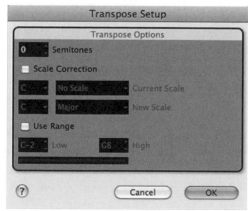

Figure 3.7: The Transpose Setup window

Using the Transpose Setup Window

For more demanding Transpose results, there's the Transpose Setup window. Click on the MIDI menu and select Transpose Setup, as shown in Figure 3.7.

Unlike the Quantize Panel, the Transpose Setup window cannot be left open at all times. Therefore, it's important to make your event selections prior to opening the Transpose Setup window. The Semitones value is identical to that of the Info Line. However, one of the most powerful transposing features of Cubase is being able to change from

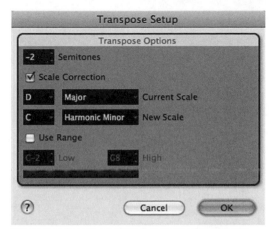

Figure 3.8: Transpose from D major to C harmonic minor

one scale to another. For example, close the window and select the Dry Finger Bass, HALion Sonic SE 01, and Rhodes events; then reopen the Transpose Setup window. Enter the values as shown in Figure 3.8.

Click on OK, and listen to the playback. You'll notice that not only have the notes been transposed, but the scale has been changed from major to harmonic minor.

Don't Transpose Drum Kit Events

Something really funny happens when you transpose drum events or tracks that have drum kit sounds assigned to them. To illustrate what I mean, Right/Ctrl-click on the SR Alta Kit and choose Select All Events from the minimenu. Then, using either the transpose value in the Info Line or the Transpose Setup window, transpose the events by 7 semitones. When you start playback, the drums sound very different. That's because when you transpose MIDI events that use drum kit sounds, the pitch of each drum sound won't change; rather, the MIDI note numbers will be transposed and change which sound is played by each note. As you can hear, the results are bizarre. The exception is if you're using a melodic percussion instrument, such as a xylophone or marimba. In those cases, transposing will function normally.

Using the Key Editor to Edit MIDI Data

When more detailed MIDI editing is needed, Cubase comes with five MIDI editors: Key Editor, In-Place Editor (a variation of the Key Editor), Drum Editor, List Editor, and Score Editor. Each editor has strengths and specific uses, but they all allow you to edit your MIDI data with microscopic precision. Before exploring the editors, make sure to read chapter 1, because you'll need to know how to select data and use zoom controls.

The Key Editor

The Key Editor is the default MIDI editor. You can access it simply by using the Object Selection tool to double-click on a MIDI event in the Event Display. (You can change the default editor in the Preferences.) You can also select a MIDI event and select Key Editor from the MIDI menu. Using either method, select the Dry Finger Bass event and open the Key Editor, as shown in Figure 3.9.

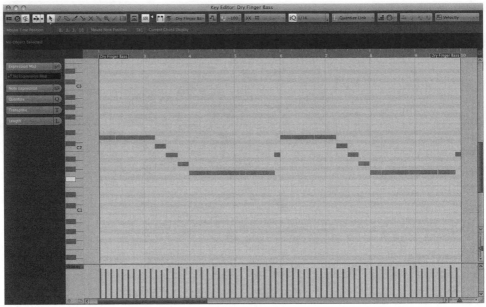

Figure 3.9: The Key Editor

You'll notice many Key Editor features with which you're already familiar from the Event Display. Features such as the Window Layout button, Toolbar, Toolbox, and many others all work in the Key Editor as they do in the Event Display. However, you'll also see some new elements, such as the Keyboard, Note Display, and Controller lane. Let's take a closer look at these new items.

The Note Display

The Note Display is very similar to the Event Display. But instead of showing events that contain the MIDI data, the Note Display shows the MIDI data itself. The little blocks you see in the Key Editor of the Dry Finger Bass are the MIDI note numbers. The vertical positions of the blocks represent the note pitch, whereas the horizontal positions represents their placement in time. The lengths of the blocks depict the note length. Since all of the notes on this event are eighth notes, the blocks are all the same size. If we were to look at a musical representation of this MIDI data, it would look like Figure 3.10.

Figure 3.10: Notation of the Dry Finger Bass event in Figure 3.9

At this point, you might understandably be wondering why Cubase doesn't always represent MIDI data in notation. This is because Cubase is able to display more musical nuance than notation. In other words, when musicians play the notation on the page, they are not able to play it with computer precision. (If they could, it would sound boring.) Instead, through their musical and human interpretation, they interject slight variations in timing. Cubase captures the performer's interpretation with a MIDI timing resolution of 480 PPQN (Pulses Per Quarter Note). Therefore, MIDI data needs to be represented with that same level of precision. Notation simply doesn't offer that level of precision, but the Key Editor does.

Acoustic Feedback

I know you might confuse this with the feedback that occurs whenever anyone in movies or TV touches a microphone, but it's not. Rather, when Acoustic Feedback is enabled, it allows you to click on and hear the MIDI notes in the Note Display. The notes will be played in context with their corresponding note lengths and velocities. (More on velocity in a moment.) You can also click on the Keyboard to hear the notes.

The Keyboard

The Keyboard is located on the left side of the Key Editor. It is a musical keyboard rotated counterclockwise by 90 degrees and offers a melodic representation of the MIDI data. In fact, if you look closely, the grid that appears behind the Note Display has lighter and darker areas that correspond to the white and black notes of the keyboard. This makes it much easier to edit MIDI notes when they are in the middle or right-hand side of the Note Display.

A Closer Look at the Event Display and Controller Lane

To get a better idea of how the Event Display and Controller Lanes represent MIDI data, load the "MIDI R01.cpr" project from the disc that comes with this book. (See appendix A, "Using the Included Disc.") In that project, you will find one Instrument track with a short MIDI event on it. Double-click that event to open the Key Editor, as shown in Figure 3.11.

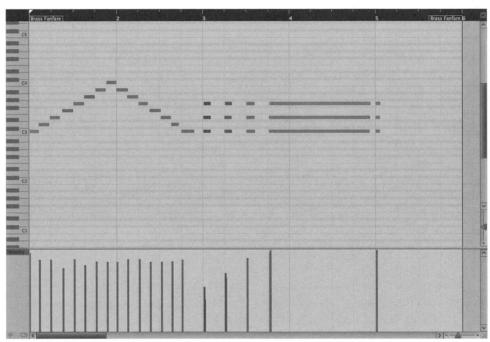

Figure 3.11: Event Display and Controller Lane of the event in the "MIDI R01.cpr" project

The MIDI notes in the Note Display start with single-note events that are similar to Figure 3.9. To the right of the single notes, you will see some stacked notes that represent chords. The notes themselves vary in color, and I'll explain why in a moment. For now, listen to the notes by starting playback. What you will hear is a C major scale followed by five C major first-position triads. The Instrument track is using a brass-section sound. The notation of the MIDI notes is shown in Figure 3.12.

Figure 3.12: Notation of the MIDI notes in Figure 3.11

Now that you've seen and heard these MIDI notes, you'll need to know how you can use the Key Editor to edit the MIDI data. The process is very similar to moving events in the Event Display. Using the Object Selection tool, you can drag notes to the left or right to alter their timing. Your Snap settings will, of course, have a lot to do with where notes can be placed. Dragging notes toward the top or bottom will alter the MIDI note number and therefore the note pitch. And as you may have surmised, dragging multiple notes up or down is yet one more way to perform a Transpose Edit.

Editing with the Info Line

The Key Editor and Event Display both have their own Info Line. If the Info Line is not visible, click on the Window Layout button (see Figure 3.9), and put a check next to Info Line. The Info Line can display very detailed information about selected MIDI events, and you can also edit those values. For example, in Figure 3.13, the Info Line is displaying the data values for the highest C note in the scale.

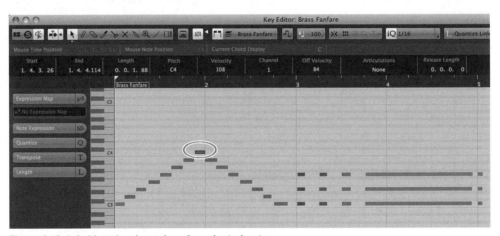

Figure 3.13: Info Line showing values for selected note

You can see the Info Line displaying timing data such as note start, end, and length values. You can also see the pitch, velocity, and MIDI channel values. You can alter any of those values to edit the selected data.

Editing MIDI Note Velocity

Velocity, or how fast the note is played, represents the note dynamics. Every MIDI note has a velocity value that is variable from 0 to 127. Values below 63 are quieter, while values above 63 are louder. It's easy to confuse velocity with volume, but be aware that they are two different things. In Cubase (and all DAW software with MIDI sequencers), velocity represents how hard the musician was playing his or her instrument, whereas volume represents the loudness of the track. Or another way to look at it is that velocity represents dynamics, such as *mezzo forte* or crescendos/decrescendos, while volume would be used to adjust the volume of the track for a fade-out.

Velocity is depicted in the Key Editor in a number of ways. We've already talked about editing the value in the Info Line, so let's explore other ways to edit velocity.

Velocity in the Note Display

As I mentioned earlier, every MIDI note in the Note Display is colorized. By default, the color represents the velocity. (See Figure 3.9, and confirm the Event Color is set to Velocity.) Quieter notes are bluer, while louder notes are redder. For example, the chords in Figure 3.11 get progressively louder. The first two chords are quieter than the following four. You can edit a note's velocity by typing Shift + Ctrl/Command while clicking on an event, and moving the mouse up and down. A small black box showing the velocity value will appear to the left of the event, as shown in Figure 3.14.

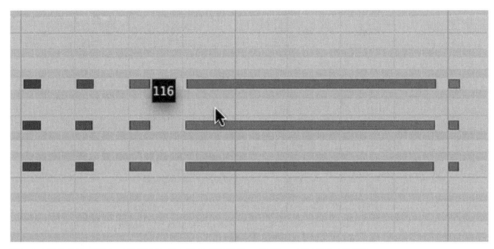

Figure 3.14: Adjusting velocity in the Note Display, velocity value box visible

Velocity in the Controller Lane

In Figures 3.9 and 3.11, you will find the Controller Lane underneath the Note Display. While MIDI velocity is not a continuous controller, the velocity values are represented here by default. The taller the vertical bars, the louder the notes. The velocity bars are also color coded identically to the notes to which they correspond in the Note Display. To edit a velocity value, use the Object Inspector to click on the vertical bar to adjust it higher or lower. Try this on the single notes in bars 1 and 2. But when you try to adjust velocity on chords, all of the notes will have their velocity values adjusted at the same time. Therefore, it's important to use the Object Selection tool to first make selections of which notes you'd like to adjust. Then velocity edits will only occur to the selected event or events, as shown in Figure 3.15.

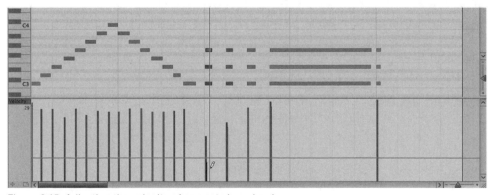

Figure 3.15: Adjusting the velocity of one note in a chord

If you have selected multiple notes in the Note Display, you can adjust multiple velocity values by clicking and dragging across the Controller Lane.

Drawing Velocity Values with the Line Tool

With multiple notes selected in the Note Display, you can select the Line tool from the Toolbox and draw a line across the Controller Lane. This will create uniform velocity values, as shown in Figure 3.16.

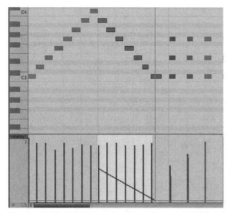 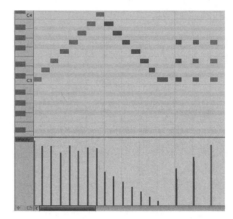

Figure 3.16: Editing velocity values with the Line tool

If a nonlinear result is desired, you can click on the Line tool icon in the Toolbox and choose from the shapes shown in Figure 3.17.

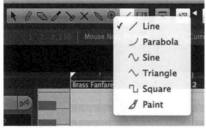

Figure 3.17: Line tool shapes

Of all the shapes, my favorite is the parabola. It is capable of creating exponential velocity curves that are very musical, whereas the default Line shape tends to create velocity curves that are a little mechanical sounding.

Editing Controllers in the Controller Lane

The Controller Lane (see Figures 3.9 and 3.11) can be used to edit a variety of different continuous MIDI data, including velocity (default), aftertouch, pitch bend, and all 128 MIDI continuous control numbers. We've already used the Controller Lane to edit velocity. Now let's explore how to edit other MIDI data.

Selecting the MIDI Controllers to Edit

At the upper-left corner of the Controller Lane, you will find the Controller Selection and Functions menu. (See Figures 3.9 and 3.11.) When you click on that menu, you will see a list of the most commonly edited MIDI controllers, along with any other controllers that currently exist on the selected event, as shown in Figure 3.18.

Notice that two of the controllers have asterisks next to them. The asterisk indicates that the controller exists on the selected event. The Brass Fanfare event we're looking at in the "MIDI R01.cpr" project contains both velocity and CC1 (Modulation) controllers. By

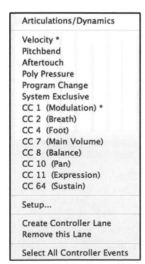

Figure 3.18: The Controller Selection and Functions menu

selecting CC1 (Modulation), the Controller Lane will show the values of the modulation data, as shown in Figure 3.19.

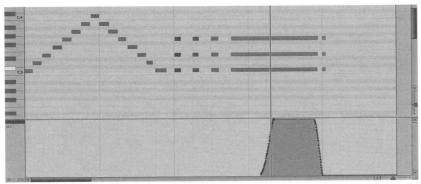

Figure 3.19: Controller Lane showing CC1 (Modulation) data

CC1 is MIDI continuous controller 1, and usually represents the movement of the modulation wheel on a MIDI keyboard controller. CC1 is used for a variety of effects, including expression, filter cutoff, and effect control, such as the speed of a rotating speaker effect. However, the most common use of CC1 is to modulate the strength of a synthesizer's LFO (Low Frequency Oscillator) to create vibrato or tremolo effects. When you start playback on the project, you'll hear the vibrato added to the brass sound throughout measure 4. This CC1 data was created at the time of recording. But now you could use either the Draw or Line tools to edit the data or create new data from scratch. Be aware that most controllers (such as CC1) start at 0 and end at 127, while others have a midpoint (such as MIDI pan, not to be confused with Peter Pan) that starts with 0 in the middle of the Controller Lane.

The In-Place Editor to Edit MIDI Data

Now that you know how to use the Key Editor, using the In-Place Editor is a breeze. It is a smaller version of the Key Editor and is located in the Event Display. Each MIDI and Instrument track has an Edit In-Place button, as shown in Figure 3.20.

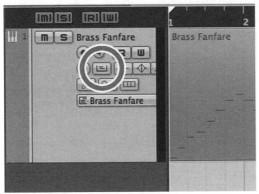

Figure 3.20: The Edit In-Place button

Be aware that the track height might need to be adjusted to reveal the Edit In-Place button. Alternately, you can select the desired track and click the MIDI menu and select Open In-Place Editor.

Using the In-Place Editor

The biggest advantage of the In-Place Editor is that you don't have to leave the Project window to edit MIDI data. And since it looks and functions exactly like the Key Editor, you needn't learn a new editor, nor close the Key Editor window. The track height will be automatically increased to accommodate the In-Place Editor, as shown in Figure 3.21.

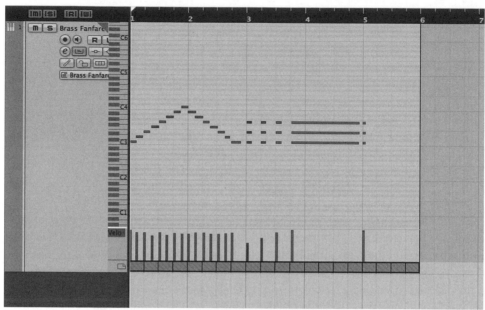

Figure 3.21: The In-Place Editor

Since the In-Place Editor is part of the Project window, you can use those tools to make edits. However, the zooming and other visual adjustments of the In-Place Editor are not quite as fully featured as is the Key Editor, and the size might make precision editing more challenging.

Other MIDI Editing Commands

Edits such as quantizing and transposition are some of the most common MIDI editing commands. However, Cubase has many others, and I'd like to show you a few that I think you'll find useful. For this section, I would recommend loading "The Right Track R03.cpr" project from the disc that comes with this book. (See appendix A, "Using the Included Disc.")

Dissolve Part

This is by far one of the most powerful MIDI edits you can perform in Cubase. Since MIDI events can contain multiple note pitches on different MIDI channels, the Dissolve Part command can separate them onto their own tracks and events. A perfect example would be taking the SR Alta Kit and separating the MIDI notes onto their own tracks, thereby creating a track for each drum sound. This allows the data to be freely and discretely edited without affecting the other data in the event. (A fringe benefit for Instrument tracks is the creation of discrete Mixer channels for each drum sound. We'll discuss this more in chapter 6, "The Art of Mixing.")

Right-click on the SR Alta Kit and choose Select All Events, then click on the MIDI

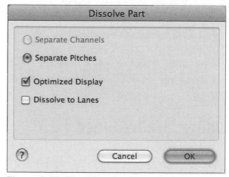

Figure 3.22: The Dissolve Part window

menu and select Dissolve Part. The Dissolve Part window will appear, allowing you to make the settings as they appear in Figure 3.22.

Make sure that Separate Pitches and Optimized Display are both selected, then click OK. The results are shown in Figure 3.23.

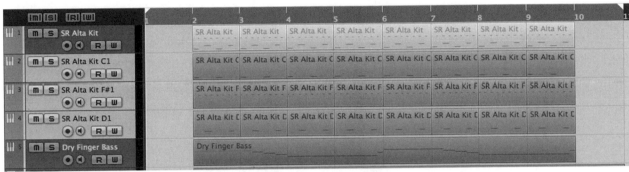

Figure 3.23: Results of the Dissolve Part command (tracks reordered for clarity)

The dissolved tracks will be placed at the bottom of the track list. I've dragged those tracks underneath the original SR Alta Kit track to make the results more clear. As you can see, each note has been dissolved onto its own track. The original track and its events have been left intact; however, the events have been muted. This leaves them in place for future editing, but they won't be heard during playback.

Velocity

Up until this point, we've taken a "note-by-note" approach to editing note velocity. But there's also a way to make velocity edits on an event-wide or track-wide basis. Select an event (or use the Select All Events command), then click the MIDI menu, select Functions, and then select Velocity. The Velocity dialog box will appear, as shown in Figure 3.24.

There are three types of velocity editing you can choose from. The default is Add/Subtract. To add value to the velocities, enter a positive value into the Amount field. Conversely, negative values will reduce the velocities. If some notes within the event exceed the minimum (0) or maximum (127) range, their values will not be altered past the limit. However, remaining velocities will be adjusted to the desired amount.

The Compress/Expand type will either smooth a wide range of velocities or expand the velocities to create a more dynamic range. The Amount field becomes a percentage from 0 to 300. Values of less than 100 percent will compress the velocities to create a less dynamic track and are useful when the recording contains too wide a range of dynamics. Values above 100 percent will expand the velocities of a track with a narrow dynamic range, so that the differences between soft and loud dynamics are more pronounced.

The Limit type will allow you to define an Upper and Lower limit into which all the velocities will be squeezed. In other words, the louder velocities will be adjusted to but not exceed the Upper limit, while the softer velocities will be adjusted to but not exceed the Lower limit.

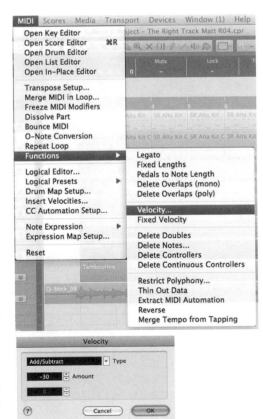

Figure 3.24: The Velocity function and dialog box

Delete Aftertouch

Aftertouch is a powerful controller. It allows the player to modulate parameters within the synthesizer even with both hands on the keyboard and both feet on the pedals. If you have a MIDI controller or keyboard with aftertouch, you may have already discovered how different sounds can be accentuated. However, you may have also noticed that many synthesizer sounds (both in Cubase and in external hardware synthesizers) don't have aftertouch assigned to a parameter, which means that pressing harder on the keys garners no results.

But the aftertouch data recorded on a track can diminish the performance of the synthesizer that's receiving it. This is because it takes more processing power to calculate the dense stream of aftertouch data. Many DAW users record aftertouch without even knowing or using it. If you start to see events that contain a lot of controller data, and you're not using aftertouch or any other controllers (such as pitch bend or modulation wheel) as shown in Figure 3.25, you might want to erase all the aftertouch. (Note: You can also set the Controller Lane Controller Selection to aftertouch to verify that the event contains superfluous aftertouch data.)

Figure 3.25: An event with a lot of possible aftertouch data

If you're not using aftertouch, you may want to remove it from specific events or even all the events within your project. Select the event (or use the Select All command to select all of the events in your project), then click the MIDI menu; select Logical Presets, standard set 2; and then del.aftertouch, as shown in Figure 3.26.

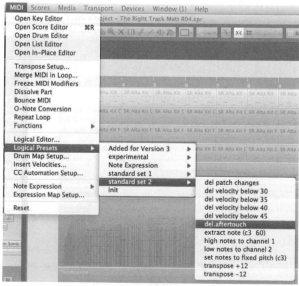

Figure 3.26: Location of the delete aftertouch command

Unlike some of the other MIDI commands, delete aftertouch has no corresponding dialog box or settings. Selecting the command simply strips all the aftertouch from selected MIDI events.

Filtering Aftertouch

If you don't use aftertouch and don't wish to have it recorded into your Cubase Project, you can enable the aftertouch MIDI filter in the Cubase Preferences. (Mac users: Click the Cubase menu and select Preferences. Windows users: Click the File menu and select Preferences.) Locate the MIDI Filters on the left side of the Preferences window, then enable the aftertouch filters in both the Record and Thru columns, as shown in Figure 3.27.

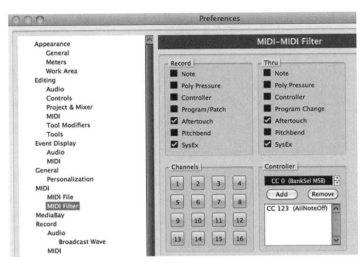

Figure 3.27: The MIDI aftertouch filter preferences

The Record filter prevents the aftertouch from being recorded, while the Thru filter prevents the aftertouch from being sent to the MIDI device, whether Cubase is in playback or stopped.

Exploring More MIDI Edits for Yourself

While perusing the MIDI menu, you undoubtedly noticed the myriad of MIDI commands, functions, and logical presets. I could write an entire book on these fascinating MIDI editing possibilities, and I urge you to explore them on your own. However, at this point, we must move on to editing audio data.

Chapter **4**

EDITING AUDIO DATA

When MIDI recording software first appeared in the mid-1980s, it ignited the fire of the digital-recording revolution. Today, the ability to not only record but edit audio data provides a creative environment that many believed would never be possible, at least not without an investment of tens of thousands of dollars. In this chapter, we'll be exploring some of those formerly impossible edits. Newer editing features such as the VariAudio pitch-correction were simply inconceivable only a few years ago. Yet today they have become an invaluable staple of modern music production.

(Note: Before reading this chapter, you should be aware that a large part of the editing process is making proper selections. Therefore, it will be very important to have read chapter 1 before proceeding further.)

We will be going over both the basics and some of the advanced editing features you'll come to rely on. For most of this chapter, we'll be using the "The Right Track Matt R04.cpr" project from the disc that came with this book. (See appendix A, "Using the Included Disc.") In this chapter, you will learn about:

- The concept of a nondestructive editor.
- The difference between online and offline processing.
- Using the Event Audio Handles.
- Crossfading Audio events.
- Pitch and time correction with the VariAudio editor.

Nondestructive and Destructive Editing

Cubase is a nondestructive audio editor. In other words, most of the edits you'll perform will not affect the actual recordings in any way. This is a very different behavior from the analog and early digital recorders. Anyone who's ever used a tape recorder or VCR (Video Cassette Recorder) understands how a destructive editor works. If you start recording on a piece of tape, any previously recorded material will be erased in favor of the new recording. And once that information is gone, there is no way of getting it back.

Examples of Destructive Editing

One famous, or rather infamous, example is the erased section of tape from (former US President) Richard Nixon's phone conversation that might have further implicated him in the Watergate scandal. Even using the most modern audio-analysis technology, that recording has never been recovered. And the cutting and splicing of analog tape is a destructive process because you are actually destroying the tape.

Early audio-editing software was the same way. Because computers didn't have the power to process the edits in real-time, the edits had to be performed on the actual audio files. In other words, if you wanted to apply a compressor to the bass drum track, you'd be destroying the original recording in favor of the compressed version. If you didn't like it, you'd need to undo it right away, because early editors did not offer unlimited undo. Rather, you'd get one undo to return the most recently processed file to its original state.

Cubase Is a Nondestructive Audio Editor

As we've previously discussed, when you record over or cut, copy, and paste in Cubase, the original material is always retained. The same is true for the commands found in the Audio menu and in the Audio Editor windows. Even though edits such as Reverse, Gain, and the VariAudio pitch correction behave like destructive editors, the original audio material is retained and replaced with processed portions that are automatically stored in the Edits folder of the Project Folder. This makes it very difficult to destroy the original recordings. It also gives you the freedom to try new things, with the confidence that you can always get back to where you started.

Offline and Online Processing

Whenever you perform an edit that appears to alter the original file, it is known as an *offline process*. In other words, Cubase magically replaces the original data with the edit but leaves the original intact. But most of the effects and other real-time processes we'll be learning about in chapters 6 and 7 can be created by the processing power of your computer and require no offline processing. As you've already guessed, adding effects such as compressors and reverbs in Cubase are known as online processes. They happen in real-time, and no additional edit files are generated.

Using the Audio Event Handles

The Audio Event Handles function identically to those found on MIDI events. You can use them to trim, add repeats, and resize the event. However, Audio Event Handles have additional functionality for adjusting the event volume, as well as fade-in and -out.

Revealing the Handles

Just like MIDI Event Handles, Audio Event Handles are revealed when your mouse is hovering over the event. But Audio events have additional handles, as shown in Figure 4.1.

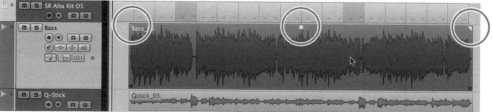

Figure 4.1: The Audio Event Handles

These handles provide a fast and convenient way to alter the volume of an Audio event. I sometimes refer to these types of edits as "QD" or quick 'n' dirty automation, because the results are similar to mix automation (see appendix B, "A Primer on Automation") but are performed on the event rather than a temporal location. But that means that copying the event will also copy the position of the handles. And while using the Mixer (see chapter 6, "The Art of Mixing") is a more robust method for volume control, sometimes you'll find an event that's just a little too loud or soft, and adjusting a handle can make an appropriate edit quickly.

Using the Volume Handle

Before you can use this method to adjust the Volume Handle, the entire scale of the event must be visible in the Event Display. (There is an alternate method I'll discuss in a moment.) With the Object Selection tool, simply click and drag the Volume Handle up or down, as shown in Figure 4.2.

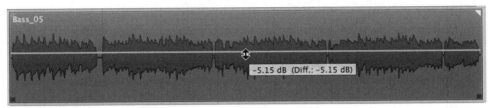

Figure 4.2: Adjusting the Volume Handle

When the adjustment is being made, a small value box will appear next to the mouse. This will indicate both the current volume value of the clip and the difference between where the handle was and where it is currently being adjusted. In Figure 4.2, the original position of the handle was 0.0 dB, but it has been moved downward to –5.15 dB. (I did that on purpose, because I love the Who song "5:15.") That's a difference of –5.15 from the original position. However, if the original position was –2 dB and adjusted to –5.15 dB, the difference would appear as –3.15 dB. When making Volume Handle adjustments, the size of the waveform will increase or decrease to help you gauge the new setting.

Be aware that you can make increment or decrement adjustments to the Volume Handle even if the value exceeds 0 dB. This is because the dynamic range of the Cubase 32-bit floating point audio engine will allow you to exceed 0 dB without clipping the Audio track. However, it still might be possible to hear distortion during playback, because the increase in event volume might cause the Master Fader (see chapter 6, "The Art of Mixing") to be clipped.

Using the Fade Handles

Unlike the Volume Handles, the Fade-in and Fade-out Handles can be adjusted without requiring that the entire event be visible. Using the Object Selection tool, click on and drag either the Fade-in or Fade-out Handle sideways. Figure 4.3 shows an adjustment to the Fade-in Handle.

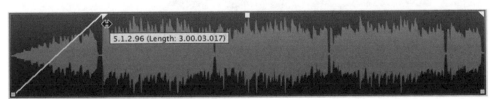

Figure 4.3: Adjusting the Fade-in Handle

When you click on a Fade Handle, the entire event will become selected. That's why Figure 4.3 and 4.2 differ in appearance. During the adjustment, a value box will display the timing of the fade. Fade-outs are created the same way, except that you'll drag the fade-out handle to the left.

Adjusting the Handles in the Info Line

If you have your Info Line visible, you can edit the fade and volume settings of a selected event, as shown in Figure 4.4.

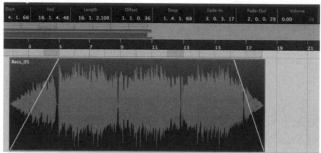

Figure 4.4: Fade and volume settings in the Info Line

This method allows you to make handle edits even when the entire event is not completely visible within the Event Display. You can single-click, double-click, or mouse wheel to adjust any value, or Alt/Option-click to edit the volume settings.

Editing the Audio Event Envelope

Every Audio event has its own volume envelope. The envelope is similar to the Volume and Fade Handles, except that you can create very dramatic volume changes at any position within the event. Since the envelope is part of the event, every paste or repeat will also retain the envelope of the original event.

Drawing the Envelope

Normally you will not see the envelope until you have edited it. That's because it is a thin horizontal line at the very top edge of the Audio event. The envelope is programmed by using the Draw tool to create points along the horizontal envelope, and then dragging those points up and down to adjust the volume, as shown in Figure 4.5.

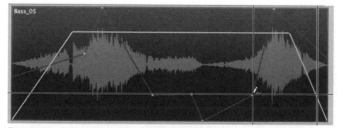

Figure 4.5: Drawing points onto the envelope

Figure 4.5 might look a little chaotic, but as you can see when editing on your color computer monitor, the handles are white while the envelope is blue. When creating new points with the Draw tool, a vertical and horizontal crosshair allows you to see the position of the point more clearly. You create new points by clicking on the envelope, or you can adjust a previously created point by clicking on it and dragging.

Crossfading Audio Events

A *crossfade* is a quick fade from one Audio event to an adjoining Audio event, which can smooth out the audible transition. When joining Audio events together, you may get lucky and not have to apply a crossfade. However, if either or both events contain anything other than almost complete silence, there's every likelihood that a crossfade will be required.

Setting Up the Crossfade Scenario

The need for crossfading will usually manifest itself as a popping, clicking, or other audible anomaly that occurs when playing through one event to another. Other times, the transition will not generate any anomalies but might just sound clumsy. Using the "The Right Track Matt R04.cpr" project from the disc that came with this book (see appendix A, "Using the Included Disc"), we're going to create an edit that will require a crossfade. Load that project, then find the event named "Bass_05" on the Bass track.

Increasing the track height as I have in Figure 4.6 will make the editing easier. Then using the Split tool and with Snap set to bar, click on the "Bass_05" event at measures 5, 9, 13, and 17, as shown in Figure 4.6.

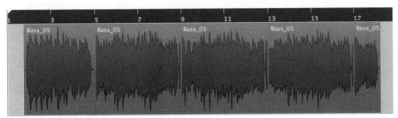

Figure 4.6: Results of using the Split tool

You have now divided the "Bass_05" event into five separate events. Using the Erase tool, click on the second event. That will result in a gap between measures 5 and 7. Now, using the Object Selection tool, press and hold the Alt/Option key on your computer keyboard and click and drag the fourth event. Drag that event to measure 5, and release the mouse. That will copy the fourth event into the gap where the second event used to exist. Refer to Figure 4.7 for more details.

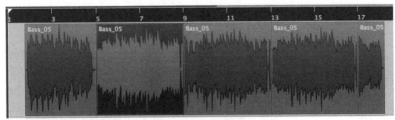

Figure 4.7: Results of copying event #4

How Pops and Other Anomalies Occur

Now solo the Bass track and start playback from measure 2 or 3 to audition the transition at measure 5. You'll notice that there are two anomalies: a pop, and it just sounds clumsy. The pop occurs because the waveforms between event #1 and the copy of #4 create a jagged transition. If you zoom in very closely, you can see that quite a portion of event #1 runs directly into a louder portion of copy of event #4, as shown in Figure 4.8.

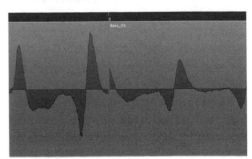

Figure 4.8: The jagged transition between event #1 and copy of #4

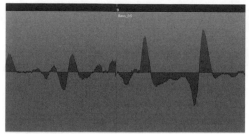

Figure 4.9: A lucky event transition at measure 9

In a perfect world, the events would always join together at what's called a *zero-crossing*. That is when both waveforms meet with complete silence on each end. This does occur from time to time, as it does when you listen to the transition at measure 9. Luckily, the waveforms of the copy of event #4 and event #3 join together at almost completely silent locations, as shown in Figure 4.9.

Because the transition is so smooth, there is no audible popping, and the edit doesn't sound clumsy like it does at measure 5.

How Clumsy-Sounding Edits Occur

Even without popping or other audible glitches, it's still possible that the transition from one event to another just sounds weird or clumsy. This normally occurs when the event you're copying is different from the one you're replacing it with. Sometimes it's caused by a difference in timing, while other times there's a slight difference in the performance. It's the latter that causes our clumsy-sounding edit in Figure 4.8. In other words, the performances in event #2 and the copy of event #4 are not identical. (If they were, you wouldn't be editing them in the first place, right?) To hear what I'm talking about, you can hit Undo a few times until event #2 is returned to its original position, and listen to the differences between #2 and #4. Then Redo until the copy of event #4 is back at measure 5.

Setting Up the Crossfade

Whether it's caused by a jagged or a clumsy transition, we're going to need to crossfade the end of event #1 into the start of the copy of event #4. Doing so will create a virtual zero-crossing and make the transition much more pleasing to listen to.

Overlapping the Events

You've already learned that Audio events cannot overlap. If they do, only the topmost event will be audible. But crossfading the events will make them both audible for a very short period of time. So what you'll do now is use the Object Selection tool to click and drag the left Event Handle of the copy of event #4 over the end of event #1. But before you do, you'll need to disable Snap by typing "J" on your computer keyboard or holding the Ctrl/Command key while dragging. Drag the handle so that it overlaps the waveform in event #1. The before and after of this procedure is shown in Figures 4.10 and 4.11.

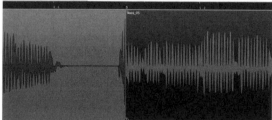

Figure 4.10: Before overlapping the events

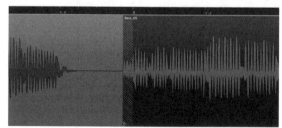

Figure 4.11: After overlapping the events

The idea is to drag the event to overlap a very brief region. However, you can see in Figure 4.10 that event #1 has a little bit of audio data that precedes the copy of event #4. So dragging the handle over this audio data will create an edit that most closely resembles the transition between event #1 and the original event #2.

Executing the Crossfade

Making the proper selection prior to executing the crossfade is critical. If you leave the only the copy of event #4 selected as it is in Figure 4.11, then crossfades will be applied to all the adjoining events, including #1 and #3. But we know that we don't need a crossfade between the copy of #4 and #3 as shown in Figure 4.9. What we want is a crossfade at measure 5 only. So use the Object Selection tool and click on event #1, then hold Shift on your computer keyboard and click on the copy of event #4. That will select both events, as shown in Figure 4.12.

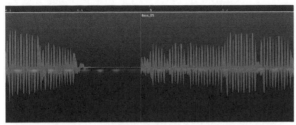

Figure 4.12: Both events selected

Now that both events are selected, type "X" on your computer keyboard. Alternately, you could choose Crossfade from the Audio menu, but hitting the "X" key is faster and resembles the shape of a crossfade, as shown in Figure 4.13.

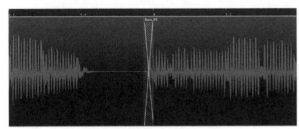

Figure 4.13: Results of the Crossfade command

You can see that the crossfade creates a short fade-in and a short fade-out, thereby creating a virtual zero-crossing at the center of the crossfade. When you listen to the crossfade, you'll notice that the transition is void of popping and sounds less clumsy. (It was me playing bass, so it cannot be completely void of clumsiness.)

Editing the Crossfade

After the events have been crossfaded, you can make further edits to the placement of the event boundaries. However, the handles with which you would normally do this are no longer visible within the crossfaded zone. But now you can simply hover your mouse over either clip boundary inside the crossfade zone, and your pointer will turn into a horizontal arrows icon. Then click and drag the boundary sideways to adjust the event boundary, and you'll notice that the crossfade will adjust accordingly.

Pitch and Time Correction with VariAudio

There was a time when singing a bad note during an otherwise brilliant vocal recording required the section to be sung all over again. But ever since the late 1990s, there has been hardware and software that makes pitch correction possible. Today, the practice of pitch correction is as ubiquitous as double-tracking and the application of reverb. In fact, it has created a whole new class of audio editing known as Auto-Tune or autotuning, named after the first commercially successful pitch-correction product from Antares Audio Technologies. Autotuning used to be performed on only the noticeably out-of-tune vocal notes. But over the past decade, producers started autotuning an entire performance to create a very synthetic vocal quality. It all started with the hit song "Believe" by Cher, and whether you love autotuning or not, it has become a very popular effect.

Autotuning of pitches is similar to quantizing MIDI data, in that if you apply too much of it, the result will be a very sterile and boring version of the original. Both techniques can literally strip all the humanity from a recording. That's why many producers (such as yours truly) prefer to use it sparingly and only when absolutely necessary. A really good singer will rarely, if ever, need to be pitch corrected. However, as every studio owner can attest, if you feel like the performance can be enhanced or if the person paying for the studio time is asking for more and more pitch correction, you'd better acquiesce to his or her request. Either way, Cubase (the full version) comes with a fantastic pitch- and time-correction editor known as VariAudio. It can provide pitch and timing effects either gently or very strictly. In this section, I'll show you how to do both.

Pitch Correction Requirements

Before you can start using VariAudio (or the vast majority of other pitch-correction programs), you'll need to be aware that the audio data must be *monophonic*. That's not to be confused with mono Audio tracks, because VariAudio can be used on Stereo tracks as well. What I mean by monophonic in this case is that the event being edited must contain recordings of only single notes without chords or overlapping notes. Examples of monophonic musical instruments are a human voice; a woodwind instrument, such as a clarinet or saxophone; or a brass instrument, such as a trumpet or French horn. However, as long as a polyphonic instrument (such as a guitar or violin) is only playing one note at a time, it too can be pitch corrected.

For the rest of this section, we'll be using the "The Right Track Matt R05.cpr" project located on the disc that came with this book. (See appendix A, "Using the Included Disc.") In that project, you will find a vocal track that has some pitch issues. I sang them that way on purpose with this exercise in mind. (Really, I did!)

Opening VariAudio in the Sample Editor

The Sample Editor is very similar to the Key Editor. But instead of editing MIDI data, it's used to edit audio data. Start by locating the event called "Vox_19" located on the Vox track (track 10) of the project. Then double-click to open the Sample Editor, as shown in Figure 4.14.

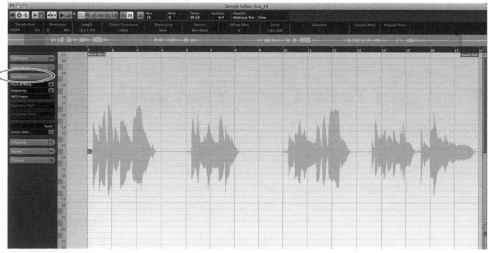

Figure 4.14: The Sample Editor and VariAudio tab

As you can see, many of the features from the Project window and Key Editor are present in the Sample Editor. It too has an Inspector, Window Layout button, and Toolbar, among others. Click the Window Layout button and make sure that the Inspector, Info, and Overview Lines are visible. Then click on the VariAudio tab in the Inspector to reveal the controls for the pitch and time correction.

Figure 4.15: The VariAudio tab

The Waveform Display will depict a lightly shaded version of the audio data. Go ahead and use the vertical and horizontal Zoom controllers to adjust the size of the waveform so that it appears as it does in Figure 4.14. Then notice that there is a vertical musical keyboard to the left of the Waveform Display. Now let's take a closer look at the VariAudio tab in the Inspector, as shown in Figure 4.15.

In the Toolbar, you will find the Solo Editor button. This will automatically solo the event during playback so that only the event you're editing will be heard. You'll also find the Acoustic Feedback button that will allow the pitches to be heard during editing. Make sure that both of those buttons are enabled.

Then there are two main tools you'll be using for VariAudio editing: the Pitch & Warp tool and the Segments tool. You'll need to switch back and forth between these tools on a regular basis, which you can do by clicking on the desired tool or typing the Tab key on your computer keyboard. For now, click on the Pitch & Warp tool. You will see a progress bar appear on the screen that depicts how long the pitch analysis will take. Longer events and longer audio files will require more time to complete. When finished, you'll see a series of segments added to the waveform display, as shown in Figure 4.16.

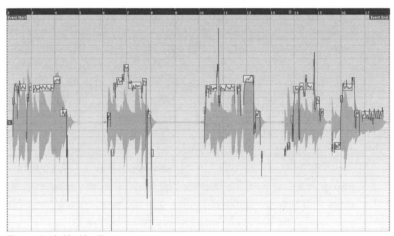

Figure 4.16: VariAudio segments

These segments depict the pitch, length, and placement of every detected syllable within the "Vox_19" event. Start playback, and watch as the cursor moves across the segments. This will give you a better understanding of what the segments represent. Because the Solo Editor is enabled, you will only hear the vocal event during playback, even if the track Solo button is not engaged.

Most of the pitches in this vocal track are tolerable. However, when you get to the third line that says, "You cannot say you know how I feel" at measure 10, you'll notice that the "I" is very (okay, I'll say it: painfully) out of tune. This is the problem note we're going to correct, and it's a doozy. Not only is it out of tune, but the pitch drifts from flat to sharp. (Did I mention I sang it this way on purpose?) Using your favorite method for zooming, zoom in so that the entire vocal line from measures 10 through 12 are visible in the Waveform Display, as shown in Figure 4.17.

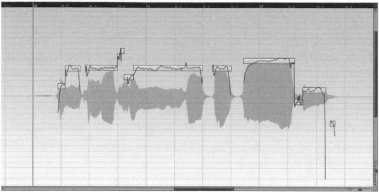

Figure 4.17: "You cannot say you know how I feel"

Using the Pitch & Warp Tool

If you look closely at the "I" segment, you'll notice that the analysis detected that it is almost a G but that it is slightly sharp. You can get a better idea of the pitch analysis by hovering your mouse over the segment. When you do, a slightly opaque vertical keyboard will become visible, as shown in Figure 4.18.

When you click on the segment with the Pitch & Warp tool, you'll be able to hear the note. That's because the Acoustic Feedback is enabled. (See Figure 4.15.) Now click and drag the segment down, and it will snap to the G. (You may get a small message in an orange border telling you that the algorithm has switched to Solo-Standard mode. This is normal because VariAudio uses that mode to shift pitches properly.) But before letting go of the mouse button, take a look at the Micro-pitch curves in Figure 4.19.

The Micro-pitch curves show how the pitch of a segment changes over time. When the event is first analyzed for pitch, you will only see the black or current pitch. But when you click and drag a note with the Pitch & Warp tool, the orange or original pitch will also be displayed. This gives you an idea of how far you're altering the pitch from its original position.

Now that the segment has been placed on G, it sounds a lot better than when it was sharper. But the segment snapped there automatically, and it's possible that an adjustment in between G and F♯ might sound better. To make finer adjustments with the Pitch & Warp tool, hold the Shift key during the edit. That will disable the chromatic snapping. You may also have noticed that the segment colors will change depending upon which note they're currently placed on. This color coding helps you see the pitch of each segment.

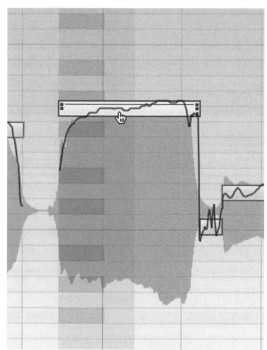

Figure 4.18: Mouse hovering over segment to reveal keyboard

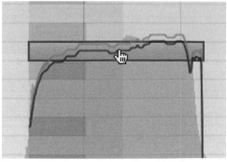

Figure 4.19: Orange (original) and black (current) Micro-pitch curves

Altering the Micro-Pitch Tilt

A simple adjustment like the one you just made might be all the editing you have to do to make the note sound properly intonated. However, you and I are not so lucky, because this segment drifts from in tune to sharp. To correct the intonation, we'll need to adjust the tilt. The Tilt control is located at the top of every segment and is much easier to see when the segment height is increased with the vertical Zoom controller. Now take a look at the "I" segment in Figure 4.20.

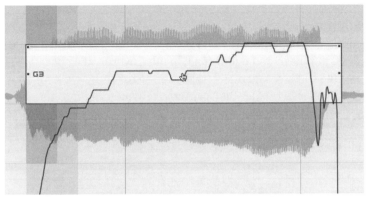

Figure 4.20: The Tilt controls

A fringe benefit of the increased segment height is that you'll be able to see both the note value and fine-tuning of the segment during editing. But now we can really see the Tilt controls represented by a thin horizontal line with small handles at the left and right. The tilt will allow you to correct the drift in pitch that the Micro-pitch curve represents in this segment. One way to adjust the tilt is to hover your mouse over one of the handles and drag up and down. Since the start of the segment is flat, click on the left handle and drag up. Then, since the note gets sharper, click on the right handle and drag down. The Micro-pitch curve should now appear as it does in Figure 4.21.

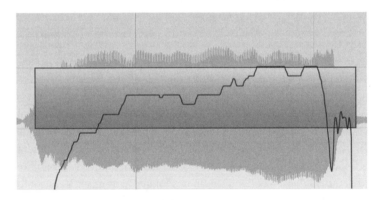

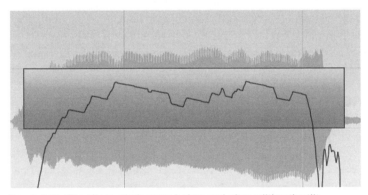

Figure 4.21: The Micro-pitch curve before and after editing the tilt

Once you've made those edits, the overall pitch of the segment might be pushed sharp or flat, requiring that you drag the segment back to G3. However, another way to adjust the tilt is to hold the Alt/Option key while moving the handle. I actually prefer this method, because the pitch of the segment is usually not altered as much as when editing either handle separately.

Straightening the Pitch

Now that the note is sounding good, there's room to make it sound better. You'll notice the Micro-pitch curve does wobble in and out of tune. In other words, the curve is not very horizontal. So using the Pitch & Warp tool, select the segment by clicking on it, then locate the Straighten Pitch slider under the VariAudio tab and drag it to the right, as shown in Figure 4.22.

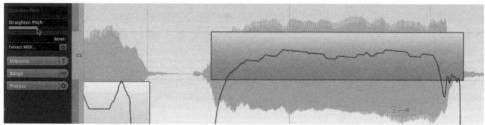

Figure 4.22: Adjusting the Straighten Pitch slider

For a segment like this, try moving the slider to about the halfway point. That will leave a bit of the human element in the segment but still improve the overall intonation of the note. When you compare Figure 4.21 to 4.22, you can see that the Micro-curve pitch has become more horizontal, therefore more in tune. I would recommend repeating this edit on the last word of the event "true." I purposely added a little "bad lounge singer" vibrato to that note, which can be easily tamed by straightening the pitch. When you listen to the playback of the entire event, you won't have to plug your ears as you run out of your studio.

Adjusting Segment Start, Stop, and Length

Another function of the Pitch & Warp tool is to make segments longer or shorter, thereby changing the note start and end positions as well as the duration. This allows you to tighten up either the start or end of a note so that it lines up with a measure, bar, or beat. (It's similar to quantizing a MIDI note, but the audio segment length is not preserved, as it would be with MIDI.) Simply click and hold on the left or right boundary of the segment, and drag sideways. The degree to which the segment can be lengthened will depend on two factors: distance and sonic quality. When making notes longer, you might eventually run into the next adjacent segment, which will define the limits to which you can lengthen the segment. But even if the segment you're lengthening has no adjacent segments, dragging the note out too long might introduce some sonic artifacts that will degrade the quality of the result. You also run the risk of making it sound humanly impossible by making the segment longer than a human's lung capacity.

Using the Segments Tool

The VariAudio analysis does an amazing job of determining syllabic content. But sometimes a singer connects words and syllables together so seamlessly that the segments are not created accurately. When this occurs, you can use the Segments tool to define the locations of those segments. That will allow you to make pitch adjustments with the Pitch & Warp tool to individual words and syllables. This is why typing the Tab key on your computer keyboard to quickly switch from the Pitch & Warp tool to the Segments tool is such a convenient way to perform VariAudio editing.

Selecting a Segment

Within the event we've been editing is "say you know," which you can see in Figure 4.17. Because there aren't any hard consonants between those words, VariAudio analyzed them as one long word. That would make it very difficult to edit the pitch or warp. So type Tab to switch to the Segments tool, and let's take a closer look at the segment we'll be editing in Figure 4.23.

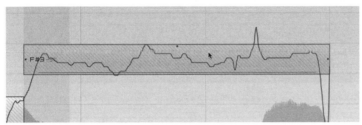

Figure 4.23: The "say you know" segment

Making the Splits

When you use the Segments tool and hover your mouse over the segment, you will see a thin horizontal line at the bottom. I haven't found a name for that line, so I'm calling it the Split line. Then move the mouse over the Split line (or toward the bottom of a segment if the Split line isn't visible due to short Vertical zoom), and the mouse turns into a Split tool icon. (It's identical to the scissors icon used by the Split tool in the Toolbox.) Now click on the Split line at the locations shown in Figure 4.24.

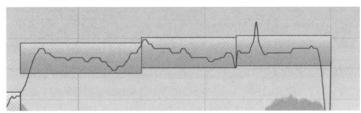

Figure 4.24: Splitting "say you know" into three segments

When you've made those splits, you'll notice that each event is moved to its newly analyzed pitch. In other words, "say" is now a little flat, "you" is properly intonated, and "know" is a little sharp. Now you can type Tab to switch back to the Pitch & Warp tool to adjust the intonation of each segment. However, just for fun, drag "you" to E3 and "know" to D3 as shown in Figure 4.25.

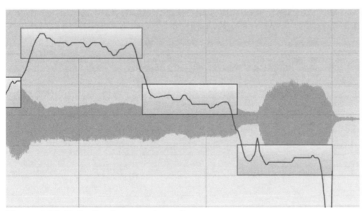

Figure 4.25: Retuning "say you know"

Now when you listen to the playback, the melody line of the phrase has been completely retuned. You may notice some character differences between the original pitches and the retuned ones. But when you listen to the vocal track in context with the rest of the tracks (and especially after we add some effects to the track in chapter 7, "Effects: Inserts, Sends, and FX Channels"), those differences will be less discernible.

Making Multisegment VariAudio Edits

Sometimes you might need to tighten up the pitch of an entire event. If you did that note by note, segment by segment, it might take a very long time. Instead, you can select multiple segments within the Sample Editor and use the Quantize Pitch and Straighten Pitch sliders to adjust all of them simultaneously. Zoom your waveform display back to how it appears in Figure 4.16. Then you can Shift-click to select multiple individual segments, or type Ctrl/Command + A to select all of the segments. For this example, select all the segments, then move the Quantize Pitch slider about halfway to the right, as shown in Figure 4.26.

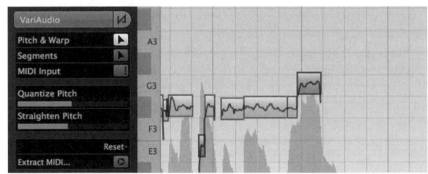

Figure 4.26: Adjusting the Quantize Pitch and Straighten Pitch sliders

You'll notice that all the segments start to move closer to their analyzed pitches. Then if you want to straighten the Micro-pitch curves, move the Straighten Pitch slider about halfway, and listen to the results. The overall intonation of the entire performance has been improved. But be aware that the accuracy of the VariAudio analysis will depend greatly on how close to the correct pitch the original recording was sung. If you notice that segments are being adjusted erroneously either sharp or flat, you'll need to use the Pitch & Warp tool to make pitch corrections to those segments individually.

Creating the "Auto-Tune" Effect

Using the same procedure outlined above in "Making Multisegment VariAudio Edits," all you need to do is move the Quantize Pitch and Straighten Pitch sliders all the way to the right. When you listen to the result and depending on your point of view, you'll be either treated or subjected to the ubiquitous Auto-Tune effect.

Beyond Pitch & Warp Editing

You've seen how you can use the Pitch & Warp tool to correct the timing of individual segments. But what happens if you want to correct rhythmic timing across multiple tracks? For that kind of editing, Cubase (the full version, 6 and above) provides Audio Quantizing and Group Editing. We'll discuss those operations in the next chapter.

Chapter 5

DRUM QUANTIZING AND GROUP EDITING

A long with pitch correction, being able to quantize multitrack drum recordings is another "holy grail" kind of editing. In a perfect world, every drummer (and all other musicians) would always practice with a metronome. That way, when they came into a recording studio and were told to play to the click track, the experience would seem more natural. Unfortunately, the world is not perfect, and many drummers find the process of recording to a click track very disconcerting. The results can be manifested as rushing, dragging, a lack of groove, and a generally sloppy-sounding drum track. A feature that first appeared in the full version of Cubase 6 is phase-accurate multitrack audio quantization. This process, in combination with Folder tracks and Group Editing can dramatically improve a multitrack drum or percussion recording. In this chapter, you will learn how to:

- Use multitrack audio quantization.
- Apply the techniques of Group Editing.
- Use Folder tracks.
- Analyze tracks for Hitpoints to detect drum notes.
- Slice, quantize, and crossfade drum tracks.
- Use the Tempo Detection feature.

Multitrack Audio Drum Quantization

For many composers, whose forte is not drumming, the simple process of quantizing MIDI drum tracks is invaluable. But when it comes to quantizing the audio recording of a real drummer, the process is not so simple. In fact, up until a few years ago, it was an extremely tedious process. But Cubase has a really fast process with which you can quantize multiple Audio tracks. Since we haven't recorded a real drum set yet, I've provided a project called "Drum Audio Quantize.cpr" that can be found on the disc that comes with this book. (See appendix A, "Using the Included Disc.") Go ahead and load that project before you continue.

Listening to the Drum Audio Quantize Project

This project is indicative of some of the timing anomalies I've mentioned. If you were to listen to it without the Click active, you might not immediately notice the timing problems. So go to the Transport menu and select Metronome Setup. (Remember, Click and Metronome are synonymous.) Make sure Metronome in Play is enabled, then click OK to close the window. If during playback you still don't hear the Click, type "C" key on your computer keyboard.

Now you can really hear how far off this drummer gets from the original tempo of 92 BPM. His performance is pretty consistent right up until measure 14, where he starts to rush. Then he has to dramatically slow down to make up for all the rushing. Then at measure 22, he's dragging behind the beat and has to rush to catch up. This is a very common problem when a drummer is changing from one drumbeat to another. What we're going to achieve by quantizing these drum tracks is a solidly and consistently timed drum recording.

When You Can Use Multitrack Audio Quantization

Before we get started, you'll need to understand the prerequisites for this type of edit. It is critical that you perform the drum quantization prior to recording any other instrumentation. This is because the other musicians are going to be listening to the recorded drum tracks, the Click, or a combination of the two while they're recording their own tracks. So if they're playing a little out of time like the drummer was during his recording, they're going to follow his prerecorded timing. Then if you quantize the drums afterward, the other tracks will suddenly sound out of time. And since you cannot quantize other instrumentation as easily as you can drums, you might find yourself in a rerecording situation that will cost you time and money.

As you can see in Figure 5.1, the "Drum Audio Quantize" project you just loaded has five tracks: Kick, Snare, Hi-Hats (Hats), Overhead Left (OH_L), and Overhead Right (OH_R).

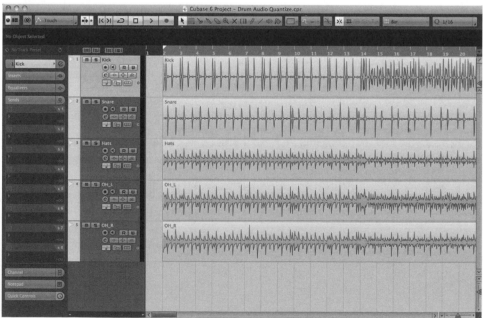

Figure 5.1: The Audio tracks in the "Drum Audio Quantize" project

All of these tracks were recorded using the contemporary method of drum recording. That is, each drum and the hi-hat cymbals were miked with a separate microphone. Then a pair of overhead microphones was placed over the drum set to capture the other cymbals and a stereo image of the entire kit. The sound from each microphone was then recorded simultaneously onto its own individual Audio track. Since drums are very percussive, each drum note is clearly visible on each track. With all of these things in mind, this project is a perfect candidate for drum quantization.

Tracks You Cannot Multitrack Quantize

Audio quantization only works on percussive tracks like drums. Therefore, other instrument recordings are ineligible for this type of editing. You simply cannot quantize tracks such as vocals, guitars, pianos, or strings, because those recordings will lack the basic principles upon which audio quantization operates: percussiveness and track separation. Therefore, tracks that contain a mix of instrumentation (such as a stereo drum track containing the entire drum recording) or that don't have clearly visible note attack (such as a bowed violin or a human voice) cannot be quantized. The bottom line is that audio quantization only works on multitrack drum recordings, such as the "Drum Audio Quantize" project.

Creating a Folder Track

A Folder track does not contain performance data like Audio or MIDI tracks. However, a Folder track can contain many, many individual tracks. Moving Audio, MIDI, or any other tracks into a Folder track can provide a multitude of benefits, including reducing visible track counts and editing multiple tracks simultaneously. It is also a requirement for multitrack audio quantization. To create a Folder track, click the Project menu, select Add Track, and then select Folder. Change the name of the track to "Drum Kit," then drag the Folder track to the top of the Track Column, as shown in Figure 5.2.

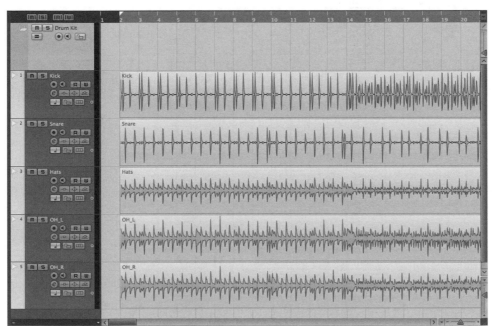

Figure 5.2: The Folder track at the top of the Track Column

I usually change the color of drum tracks to yellow (it's a long story), so I prefer to make the Folder track the same color as the tracks it will contain. This makes it easier to identify the track simply by looking at it.

Moving Tracks into a Folder Track

To move the drum tracks into the Folder track, click the Kick track, and then Shift-click the OH_R track to select them all. Then click and drag any track to the midpoint of the Folder track. You will see a vertical green arrow pointing left, as shown in Figure 5.3.

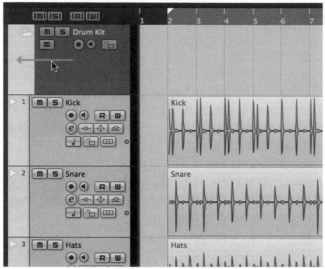

Figure 5.3: Moving the tracks into a Folder track

After you release the mouse button, the Audio tracks will be packed into the Drum Kit Folder track. The appearance of the Track Column won't be dramatically different from before. But there are two things to notice in Figure 5.4.

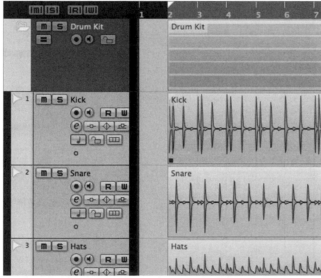

Figure 5.4: Folder track icon and horizontal indent of tracks

The folder icon has two states: open and closed. The Folder track in Figure 5.4 is open; therefore, the tracks it contains can be seen in the Track Column and the Event Display. But since those tracks are in a Folder track, they are slightly indented to the right.

Closing and Opening the Folder Track

Clicking on the folder icon will close the folder and hide the tracks it contains. You can see how closing the Folder track can dramatically reduce the visible tracks in the Track

Column. This makes it much easier to manage a project when you've added more and more tracks. When you mute the Folder track, the tracks it contains will also be muted. The same is true for Solo and other track functions such as record enable and monitor. Plus, when you use any of the tools (such as the Split or Erase tools) on the Folder track, all of the tracks inside will also be edited. You will see why this behavior is important when you start quantizing these tracks.

Another Method for Creating Folder Tracks

The reason I showed you the "long way" first was so that you could visualize the concept of a Folder track. But now that you understand the concept, let me show you a shortcut. With the desired tracks selected, click the Project menu, select Track Folding, then choose Move Selected Tracks to New Folder. While you will still need to rename and (if desired) colorize the Folder track, you won't have to reposition the track or drag the tracks into the Folder track.

Analyzing Hitpoints

Hitpoints are what Cubase uses to indicate, among other things, where musically significant events (such as drum notes) are on an Audio track. In the case of multitrack audio quantization, you will need to analyze for Hitpoints on some, but not all, tracks. I would recommend using the Kick, Snare, and one of the overhead tracks. Due to the differences in both the note quantity and volume, each track will have to be analyzed separately.

Analyzing the Kick Track for Hitpoints

Double-click the Kick event to open the Sample Editor. Click on the Hitpoints tab in the Inspector, as shown in Figure 5.5.

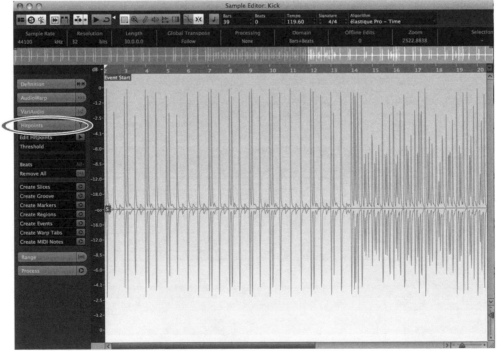

Figure 5.5: The Sample Editor and Hitpoints tab

Click the Edit Hitpoints button as shown in Figure 5.6, and watch what happens to the waveform display.

Figure 5.6: Results of the Hitpoint analysis

The vertical gray lines that appear in the waveform display will indicate where the Hitpoint analysis has detected drum notes. However, as you can see, there are a lot of them. What we want to do is refine the detection so that Hitpoints are only created for the notes that come from the kick drum. In other words, because the sound of other drum instruments will bleed into the microphone during recording, not all of the detected Hitpoints are kick drum.

Adjusting the Threshold

By default, the Threshold control (see Figure 5.7) is set to its most sensitive position. That's why even the slightest sound is detected as a kick drum note. By moving the Threshold slider to the right, you can refine the Hitpoint detection to only identify kick drum notes.

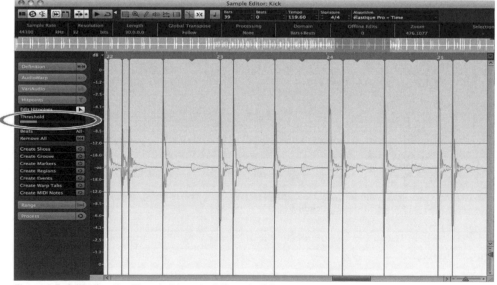

Figure 5.7: Adjusting the Threshold control (Sample Editor zoomed in)

As you adjust the Threshold, two horizontal lines will appear in the waveform display. These are the Threshold indicators, and they help you differentiate between loud notes and quiet notes. The loud notes are most probably kick drum, so you want to set the Threshold low enough that it detects the quietest kick drum. However, if you set it too low, it might detect quiet notes that are actually bleed-through from other drums. In the case of Figure 5.7, you'll notice that the kick notes have Hitpoints, while the snare notes that bleed through do not. This is an appropriate setting for the Kick event.

Analyzing Hitpoints on the Snare and OH_R Events

Now you're going to close the Sample Editor and repeat the Hitpoint detection and Threshold adjustment on the Snare and OH_R tracks. Keep in mind that the Threshold setting for the Snare will be roughly the same as it was for the Kick. However, the OH_R event will contain notes from the Kick, Snare, and any other instrument on the drum set. Therefore, the OH_R Threshold will certainly need a lower, more sensitive setting.

Group Editing

The Folder track, when compared to other tracks, does not have as many controls. However, it does have one unique control called Group Editing. It is a small button that looks like an "=" sign, as shown in Figure 5.8.

When Group Editing is enabled, it allows edits you make on one event to be applied to every event. Those events must be inside the same Folder track. Since multitrack audio quantization must be phase accurate, all the events must be edited equally. So go ahead and click the Group Editing button, but there's a catch.

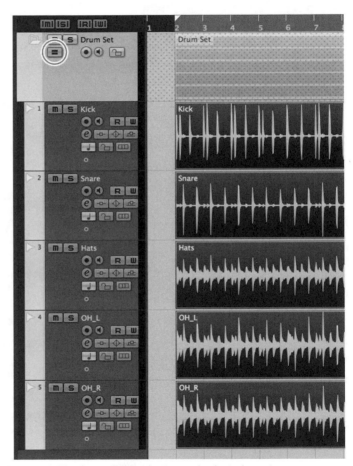

All Events Must Be Selected

For the quantization to work properly, all of the events inside the Folder track must be selected. This can be a little tricky, but I've found the quickest solution. After the Group Editing button is enabled, you simply click on any event contained within the Folder track. The selection of any event in the folder will select them all.

Other Group Editing Situations

Group Editing is the function that makes multitrack audio quantization possible. However, there are many other applications. For example, if you're simultaneously editing several tracks, such as background vocals or layered guitar tracks, Group Editing allows you to make identical edits across

Figure 5.8: The Group Editing button and selected events

all tracks. Then if you find one event that needs a little individual editing, you can disable Group Editing, perform the edit, and reenable Group Editing to pick up where you left off.

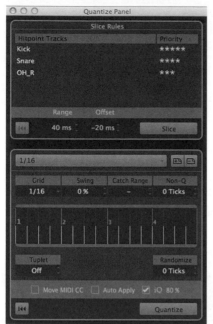

Figure 5.9: The Quantize Panel with Slice Rules (Group Editing only)

The Quantization Process

Now we're going to quantize all the drum events. This will require that you open the Quantize Panel, either by selecting it from the Edit menu or by clicking the small button to the right of the Quantize Presets at the top of the Project window. If you've seen the Quantize Panel while editing MIDI data, you'll notice that it has several more options in Group Editing mode, as shown in Figure 5.9.

The Slice Rules at the top of the Quantize Panel are only visible when you're in Group Editing mode. In the Hitpoint Tracks column, you'll see a list of the three tracks you've analyzed for Hitpoints. In the Priority column, you can change which tracks have the highest priority (more stars) or lowest priority (fewer stars). In this case, it set the priority by the order in which the events were analyzed. This order will usually garner the best results, so make sure that you follow the priority in Figure 5.9 regardless of their order during Hitpoint analysis.

Making Slices

When you click the Slice button in the Slice Rules section, you'll see that every event will get split into multiple events as shown in Figure 5.10, which is zoomed in to reveal a one-bar region at measure 14.

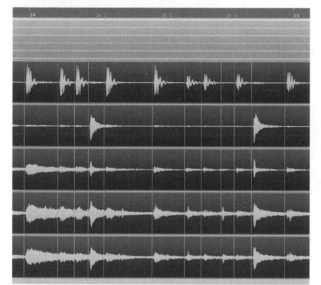
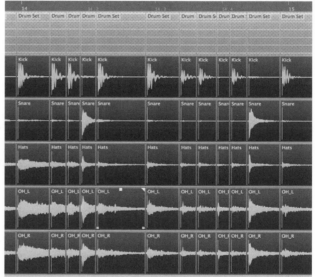

Figure 5.10: Events sliced at Hipoint locations, measure 14

If you audition the playback now, you won't notice any audible difference, because we haven't altered the timing yet. The Slice command only creates individual events for every Hitpoint across all the events. But the actual slices are not made directly at the Hitpoints. Instead, the Offset control on the Slice Rules is set at its default of –20 ms (milliseconds). That way, the initial attack of the drum note is retained, and you won't get popping or clicking due to slices made inside of the waveform. The Offset amount ensures that slices are made at quiescent parts of the event. But if you'd rather adjust where the slices are made, you can customize the amount of Offset.

Similarly, the Range control has a default of 40 ms, which ensures that the slices will be a minimum of 40 ms apart. For this example, I found that a Range setting of 80 ms garnered the best results. This was because of a few flams (notes played very close together) that created some clumsy-sounding results if they were sliced into individual events. Therefore, hit Undo (Ctrl/Command + Z), change the Range to 80 ms, and click the Slice button again.

Another tip is to consider how busy the drummer performance is. Events with a lot of Hitpoints (such as 16th notes or 32nd notes) might require a shorter Range, while events with sparse Hitpoints might require a longer Range.

Quantizing the Slices

The Quantize section of the Quantize Panel (see Figure 5.9) is identical to that of MIDI Quantize. Basically you'll need to determine an appropriate Quantize Preset based on the shortest note that was played in the recording. The shortest note in the "Drum Audio Quantize" project is a 16th note. Therefore, the 1/16 preset is the best choice. Then you can also enable iQ (Iterative Quantize) to retain a percentage of the original timing. In this example, the default of 60 percent will not garner a tight timing. This is because of how far offbeat the drumming was at certain sections. I would recommend using iQ whenever possible, but in this case, we'll need to set the percentage to around 80 percent. Then click the Quantize button, and your events should resemble those in Figure 5.11.

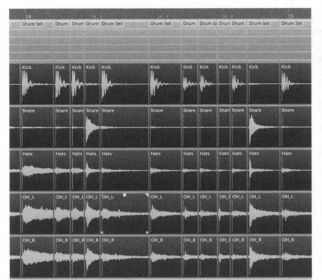
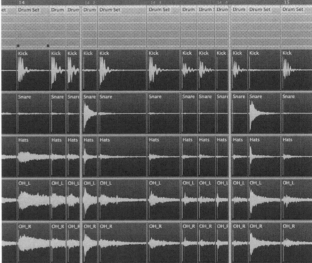

Figure 5.11: Events quantized resulting in gaps, measure 14

When you audition the playback now, the events land very closely, but not precisely to the nearest 16th note. That's due to the iQ retaining some of the human timing element. However, you'll also notice that audible and visible gaps have appeared between many of the events. That's because the quantization process moved the events forward or backward in time. Those gaps reveal the degree to which the events have been moved. So while the timing has been improved, the gaps make the playback sound choppy and stuttering. Fortunately, there's an easy remedy for this problem.

Crossfading the Slices

You may not have noticed that the Quantize Panel had some controls added to it when you clicked the Slice button. However, there's now a Crossfades section at the bottom of the Quantize Panel, as shown in Figure 5.12.

When you click the Crossfade button, you'll notice that a small crossfade will be applied across all of the events. And since Group Editing is on, the crossfades are applied to all of the tracks, as shown in Figure 5.13.

Figure 5.12: The Crossfades controls

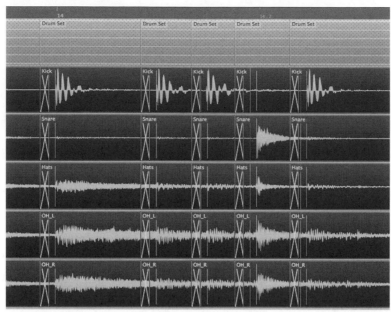

Figure 5.13: Crossfades added to all events and tracks

Now that the crossfades have removed the audible gaps from between the events, when you audition the playback, it's void of that choppy, stuttering feel, and the timing is dramatically improved. If longer or shorter crossfades are desired, you can now adjust the Length setting from the default of 22 PPQN (Pulses Per Quarter Note) or even click the Nudge buttons to reposition the crossfades. If want to further customize the crossfades, you can click the "e" button to open the Crossfade Editor. But in this example, I'm sure you'll agree that the quantization of this drum performance was a vast improvement over the original. To hear the difference, hit Undo (Ctrl/Command + Z) a few times until you return to a presliced or prequantized state, and listen to the unquantized original performance. You'll certainly prefer the quantized version.

If for any reason you got results that didn't sound good, you can load the "Drum Audio Quantize Complete" project to listen to my results and compare the Hitpoint detection results.

Tempo Detection

Cubase 6 (the full version) introduced a feature called Tempo Detection. It's similar to multitrack Audio Quantize in that it uses Hitpoint detection to determine where percussive notes occur. However, it doesn't quantize the audio. Rather, it sort of quantizes the tempo of Cubase to an audio file. This is extraordinarily useful when you receive drum tracks from another studio that were not recorded to a click track. In that case, the Tempo Detection can line up your Cubase measures, bars, and beats to the audio files. You can even try this on an audio file of a complete mix, as long as it has consistent drum transients that Tempo Detection can "see" and convert into tempo information. In fact, I love to do that by importing audio CDs of my favorite drummers into Cubase and then using Tempo Detection to see just how tightly they really play. Tempo Detection will also introduce us to two new track types: Tempo and Signature.

Tempo Detection on a Multitrack Project

If you ever find yourself getting worse results from drummers when they're trying to follow the click track, you may just need to let them record their performances using their own internal timing. But that can cause problems later when trying to reference the project timing to measures, bars, and beats. For this example, load the "Tempo Detection. cpr" project from the disc that came with this book. (See appendix A, "Using the Included Disc.") This is a recording of a drum set, and we don't know what the tempo of the song is. To see what I mean, make sure that Metronome in Play is enabled in the Metronome Setup window (Transport menu), and listen to the playback. You'll notice the Click and the tempo of the Audio tracks are not synchronous. And since these tracks weren't recorded to a click track, the timing would drift if we were to try and guess what the correct tempo might be.

Choosing a Track for Tempo Detection

As you can see in Figure 5.14, we have a project with ten tracks: Kick, Snare, Hi-Hats, four Tom Toms, and two Overheads.

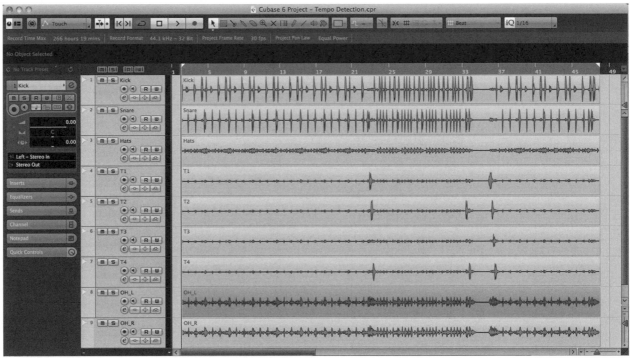

Figure 5.14: Track layout of the Tempo Detection Project

For Tempo Detection to work properly, it needs lots of percussive transients. The track in the project that fits the bill is one of the overhead tracks, such as OH_L (Overhead Left) or OH_R (Overhead Right). Since those microphones pick up the entire drum kit, they contain the most drum notes. Select the OH_L event (which I have colorized green rather than yellow to make it easier to identify), then click the Project menu, and select Tempo Detection.

Figure 5.15: The Tempo Detection panel

Analyzing the Tempo

The Tempo Detection panel has one large Analyze button along with some additional options, as shown in Figure 5.15.

The first step is to click the Analyze button. A progress bar will appear, and gives you an idea of how long the analysis will take. When complete, two new tracks will be added around the OH_L track. (See Figure 5.16.) We'll discuss the Signature track at the top in a moment. For now, let's look at the new track underneath called the Tempo track.

The Tempo Track

When you look at the data contained on the Tempo track, you will see a series of little boxes on a horizontal string. The string is the Project tempo, while the little boxes are where the Tempo Detection analysis determined the tempo changes occurred. In other words, and in a similar way to Hitpoint detection in the Sample Editor, a strong transient (such as a drum note) is identified as a Hitpoint. Then Cubase places a tempo change along the tempo line at those locations. The Tempo track is also where you can customize the tempo of your project to create tempo changes. You do this by adding a Tempo track to the project, then using the Draw tool to add your own little boxes (or as some like to call them, donuts on a rope) across the tempo line. However, let's get back to Tempo Detection.

Now when you play back the project, you'll hear that the Click and the Audio tracks are perfectly in sync. The Tempo Detection process does not alter the audio files in any way, only the Tempo track. However, you may also have noticed a few other changes that appear in Figure 5.16.

Figure 5.16: Additional features of the Tempo Detection process

The Time Ruler at the top of the Event Display is now rust colored rather than blue. That's because the Time Warp tool has been selected automatically, and when you hover your mouse over an event, it will appear as a mechanical metronome (the kind that might be sitting on your piano right now) with horizontal arrows at the top. Using that tool, you could reposition the Warp markers located in the Time Ruler to fine-tune the tempo. We won't need to do that in this example, because the Tempo Detection was nearly perfect.

Another thing to consider is the placement of the Audio tracks inside the Event Display. I put the strongest downbeat right on measure 2. This helped Cubase determine where the first Warp marker (and therefore the first Tempo change) should be placed.

The Divide and Multiply Buttons

When you listen to the playback, you'll notice that the Click sounds as though it's in double-time compared to the Audio tracks. This is a very common occurrence and very easy to fix using either the Multiply or Divide buttons on the Tempo Detection panel. (See Figure 5.15.) If the Click sounds double-time, click the Divide button. When you do, the Tempo changes are divided in half from roughly 180 BPM to 90 BPM. However, if the resulting Tempo Detection sounds half-time, you can click the Multiply button to double the Tempo changes.

The Time Signature Track

The Signature track contains any changes to the time signature. You'll notice that at measure 1, there's an establishing time signature of 4/4. (See Figure 5.16.) However, at measure 2, there's a change to 1/4. This is because the Tempo Detection places the Warp markers at what it has determined (or what it thinks) are quarter-note positions, but it doesn't know what the true time signature is. You may have also noticed that during playback, all the Clicks are high-pitched beeps. That's another reminder that you'll need to edit the Signature track to establish the proper time signature.

Before you can edit the time signatures, you will need to close the Tempo Detection dialog. Then, since these tracks are 4/4, you'll have to switch to the Object Selection tool and change the second time-signature change, double-clicking the value and typing in "4/4." (See Figure 5.17 for more detail.)

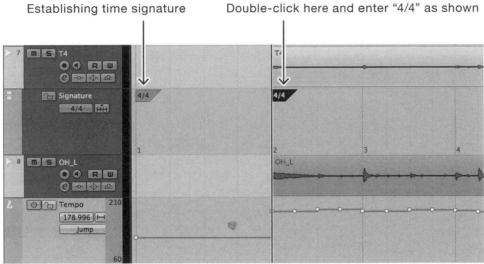

Figure 5.17: Editing the time signature

Now that the project has the proper tempo and time signatures, you'll notice that the Click and the audio playback are solidly synchronized. This will allow you to more easily edit the tracks and events, and you can reference the current position to measures, bars, and beats.

Getting into the Mix

Now that we've added a bunch of new editing skills to our Cubase repertoire, we can start mixing and adding effects and EQ, and editing a mixdown of a project. Now might be a good time to go pour yourself a tall, refreshing beverage, because the next series of chapters are going to get intense.

Chapter 6

THE ART OF MIXING

Mixing music is, indeed, an art form. Hopefully, you're not intimidated by that fact. You see, there are many types of art and different levels of artistic expression. The masters of the visual arts did not create their most famous masterpieces on their first day. It took Vermeer nearly a decade of work before he painted *Girl with a Pearl Earring*, and Rodin sculpted *The Thinker* late in his career. Whether you're a sculptor, painter, or music maker, you have to start your art somewhere. And believe it or not, making professional-sounding mixes is easier than you think. In this chapter, you will learn:

- The "Big Three" actions for a professional mix.
- How to use the Cubase Mixer.
- How to adjust volumes and use Group tracks.
- How to make a more spacious mix with the Pan controls.
- How to make tracks more audibly legible with EQ (equalization).
- The concept and importance of the Master Fader.

A Word About Buffer Settings

When you get to the mixing phase of your project, it means you're done recording new tracks. So the buffer settings that control your latency don't need to be as low. In fact, low buffer settings can be problematic at this point. That's because the mixing process usually involves adding components such as EQ and effects that require more processing power to create. Low buffer settings may not allow enough time for the computer to generate these processor-intensive effects. The results will usually be manifested as pops, clicks, dropouts and distortion. To prevent those anomalies and distractions, make sure to increase your buffer settings. See appendix C, "Managing Audio Interface Buffer Settings," for detailed instructions.

The "Big Three" Actions for a Professional Mix

When I said that mixing is easier than you think, you might have thought that too bold a statement. Certainly the art of mixing requires a multifaceted approach developed through years of training and experience. But the basic goal of mixing is this: making every recorded sound audible. Granted, that task is a very challenging one, especially when you start adding a lot of tracks to a project. In other words, it's usually easier to mix one singer and one piano than it is to mix an entire pop band. However, regardless of the track count, musical genre, or instrumentation, there are three basic actions required to make a balanced professional mix: loudness, direction, and focus. Translated into Cubase terms, I'm talking about volume, pan, and EQ (equalization or tonal control).

Action 1: Controlling Loudness with Volume

Regardless of how much mixing you've done, you're probably familiar with the Channel Fader, either in Cubase or on a physical mixer. The Fader controls the volume of whatever is plugged into that channel. In the case of Cubase, the Channel Fader controls the volume of the MIDI, Instrument, or Audio track you've recorded. In the early days of audio mixers, the Faders were usually knobs or levers and resembled the laboratory set from the 1931 film *Frankenstein*. They weren't very elegant looking, but they did what they were designed to do: make volume adjustments.

The same is true for the Channel Faders in Cubase. If a track is too quiet, turn up the Fader. If it's too loud, turn the Fader down. It's important to realize that Faders go down as well as up. Therefore, turning some Faders down can make other tracks more audible.

Action 2: Controlling Direction with Pan

Early audio recordings were done in mono. That is, the sound was recorded with one microphone and played back through one speaker. But humans have two ears, one on each side of our heads, which allows us to hear in stereo. To make that possible, our brain processes the sound coming through our left ear separately from the sound coming through our right ear. This gives us an idea of where the sound is coming from. Early humans used their stereoscopic auditory senses to determine where the sounds of a ferocious and hungry animal were coming from. Today, we use them to avoid being hit by a passing automobile. (That is, unless we have our earbuds cranked to 110 dB as we walk obliviously down the sidewalk.)

But we also listen to music stereoscopically. Even before there was any recording equipment, humans went to musical performances and enjoyed being able to hear every instrument of a full orchestra. The layout of the instrumentation on stage made it much easier for human ears and brains to process all the different sounds. The violins and violas sat stage right and were perceived by the left ear, while the celli and basses sat stage left and were perceived by the right ear. If all of the musicians were placed at center stage, the sound would essentially be monophonic, and it would be much more difficult to hear individual instruments. (I'm sure that would violate some union rules, but I digress.)

When stereo recording became possible, it meant that stereo microphones were placed in front of the orchestra and then played through separate left and right speakers. As pop music hit the scene, a full band was recorded in much the same way. But then multitracking allowed every instrument to be recorded onto its own discrete track. So how do you simulate a natural stereophonic environment with a series of monophonic tracks?

The answer is the Pan control. *Pan* is short for panorama, or the perception of sounds from different directions. By taking a track and panning it to the left or the right, you're able to send the signal to the listener's left or right ear. The result is a much more pleasing and spatial mix. In fact, you'll find that if you can't adequately balance a series of tracks with volume control, spreading them across the stereo landscape with the Pan control can instantly create audibility. Whether we know it or not, the direction from which the sound is coming is constantly being analyzed by our ears and brains.

Ideas for Pan Control Settings

I work with a lot of recordings from people who hire me to mix their music. Many of them have given it their best effort, but they usually tell me, "We tried, but we just can't make it sound right." Believe it or not, many of the Cubase or Nuendo (Steinberg's audio-post DAW program) projects I receive have the tracks all panned center. That renders the mix monophonic, and it's no wonder the results to that point have been dissatisfying. So let me share with you some ideas on where tracks should be panned.

If you're recording a symphony orchestra in a multitrack fashion (separate instruments or sections on separate tracks), the positions of the Pan controls are pretty easy. Basically, you'd be replicating the layout of instrumentation on the stage. But solo instruments are quite different. For example, when a piano is played, the performer hears the low strings in his or her left ear, middle notes in both ears, and high strings in his or her right ear. But when we hear the piano played at a concert or recital, we don't perceive the instrument in the same way, because the piano is usually turned perpendicular to the audience. The best way to handle this situation is to listen carefully to a wide pan (player perspective) or a narrow pan (audience perspective) and decide which sounds better. You can also ask the performers which method they prefer.

Things get even more challenging with pop bands. What I mean by "pop" is a band with combo-style instrumentation, such as drums, guitars, piano, brass, turntables and/or vocals. This could be a country, rock, hip-hop, or jazz band. If the band has a drum set, you'd simply duplicate the listener's perspective. In other words, for a right-handed drummer, the bass drum would be center, the high tom would be panned toward the right, the floor tom would be panned toward the left, and so on. However, I have found some drummers who prefer to have their mix panned player-perspective rather than audience-perspective. It's a good idea to ask them which they like. But the other instrumentation is almost as easy to determine if you ask the question, "Which side of the stage do you stand on during a performance?"

For example, let's say I was recording a rock band like AC/DC. (I reserve the right to dream at any time.) We already know how the drums will be panned. Then Brian Johnson (vocals) stands mostly center stage. Cliff Williams (bass guitar) stands slightly to audience right of Phil Rudd (drums). Then Malcolm Young (rhythm guitar) stands on audience left, while Angus Young (lead guitar) stands (rather, flails) on audience right. If you have any AC/DC in your music library, take a listen to it. You'll find that their stage layout is precisely re-created on their studio recordings. If you have trouble hearing what I'm talking about, use headphones and only put one cup (or ear bud) on at a time.

Of course, the "where do you stand" method should not be treated as a rule but rather a guideline. There are plenty of recorded examples where this method wasn't employed. Take any Van Halen album, especially the early ones. Even though Eddie Van Halen stood on audience right, his guitars (except for most solos and intros) are panned hard audience left. It's really strange to listen to "Runnin' with the Devil" with only the right headphone on, because you won't hear any guitar (except for the reverb) until the solo. I still don't know why (producer) Ted Templeman did it that way. I can only assume that Eddie wanted to be heard more from the driver's side of a car stereo. (And since Van Halen fans like me never had a date to sit in the passenger seat . . . oh, nevermind.)

Action 3: Controlling Focus with EQ

Focus is a little hard to describe in audio terms. Instead, I'll use the metaphor of photography. Imagine you're trying to photograph a bear at some distance from you in the woods. You'll need a long telephoto lens to increase the size of the bear for the proper photographic composition. Long lenses have a much deeper range of focal points. Because of this, let's pretend that the foreground is filled with trees, which the camera autofocus is mistakenly presuming to be the subject of your photograph. In other words, the trees are in focus, while the bear is out of focus. To cure this situation, you'd turn off autofocus and manually move the focus past the trees and toward the bear instead.

Now let's explore this metaphor in audio terms. If you have a lot of foreground tracks, especially instruments that compete for the same tonal space (such as vocals and rock guitars), it becomes very challenging to make all the tracks heard by using volume or pan alone. Background instrumentation can be just as important as foreground tracks. So in situations like these, you'll need tonal control, which Cubase refers to as equalization and I refer to as EQ. Either way, they're synonymous.

We'll be going through some practical examples of EQ later in this chapter. But I want to leave you with this concept: EQ is a specialized volume control. A Channel Fader adjusts the overall track volume; however, an EQ adjusts the volume of certain frequencies. With EQ, you can accentuate the signature "voice" of a track, which might include emphasizing the volume of certain frequencies or deemphasizing the volume of others. The result is that you can use EQ to bring both foreground and background instrumentation into proper audio focus.

Introduction to the Cubase Mixer Controls

Before we start using the Mixer, we need to understand its controls and the myriad of different places we can find them. We also need to understand the identical natures of a physical mixer and the Cubase Mixer. They both collect a series of audio signals and blend them together to create something rich and wonderful for other humans to listen to.

In an analog or digital tape–based studio, the physical mixer, more than the tape machines, is the centerpiece of the control room. An example of which can be seen in Figure 6.1.

Figure 6.1: A tape-based digital recording studio, circa 1999

For the perspective client, the supposition was: the bigger the mixer, the more "pro" the studio. Therefore, it was common for studio owners to purchase not only the mixer they needed but as much mixer as they could afford. The size of the mixer was a critical component of the recording studio and also a great marketing tool.

Now that DAW software is the de facto standard for audio recording, the physical mixer has been reproduced in software. The Mixer in Cubase largely replaces a physical mixer, but it can also do things that physical mixers cannot, regardless of cost. Features such as fader automation, multiple aux sends, multiple effect returns, and 4-band equalizers on every channel were usually only found on the most expensive of mixers (literally tens, if not hundreds, of thousands of dollars). Today, the Cubase Mixer has all of those features and more.

Before we can get into the details of the Mixer, you will have to load an existing project, or start a new empty project and add at least one Audio track.

The Mixer and the Inspector

I know that sounds like an early '70s British comedy, but what I'm talking about is the basic mixing functionality found in the Inspector. For every MIDI, Instrument, Audio, Group, and FX Channel track (the latter two of which we'll discuss later), there are Inserts, Equalizers, Sends, and Channel tabs, as shown in Figure 6.2.

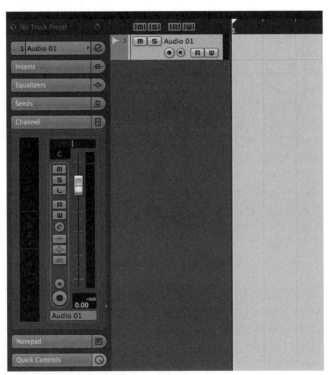

Figure 6.2: Inspector tabs for mixing

Basically, the Inspector can display the most commonly used mixing controls on any selected track. That means that a lot of the controls can be accessed directly from the Project window without having to go to the Cubase Mixer. We'll discuss what all of these Mixer features are used for as we go along, but let's take a look at other ways to access them.

The VST Channel Settings

Clicking the Edit button (see Figure 6.2) will open the VST Channel Settings window for the selected track. It contains the same Mixer controls as the Inspector tabs, but it displays them all simultaneously, as shown in Figure 6.3.

Figure 6.3: The VST Channel Settings window

The VST Channel Settings window can be thought of as a "channel strip." If you've ever used a physical mixer, the controls closest to you are the faders. Then above the faders are a series of knobs for EQ (equalization), aux (auxiliary) sends, and input gain. That tall row of controls from the fader to the input knob is known as a channel strip, and the signal flows from top to bottom. However, Cubase does not display the channel strip in the same way. If it did, you'd need a computer screen that's about twice as tall as the one you have. Instead, Cubase arranges the controls from left to right, with Inserts on the far left, followed by the Equalizers, Sends, and Channel Fader. And instead of the signal flowing from top to bottom, it flows left to right. In other words, the sound from the track flows through the Inserts, then into the Equalizers, then to the Sends, and finally to the Channel Fader. This signal flow is very important to understand, and we'll discuss why later. But bear in mind that the signal flow in Cubase is identical to that of a traditional analog mixer.

The Cubase Mixer

The Cubase Mixer is used almost nearly as much as the Project window, especially once you start the mixing process. It's so important that many Cubase users (myself included) invest in a second computer monitor display upon which to permanently place the Mixer. (If you want to add another monitor display, make sure its screen resolution is at least 1024 x 768 pixels [XGA] to accommodate the full height of the Mixer.)

The Basic or Fader Mixer View

Go to the Devices menu and select Mixer, or type F3 on your computer keyboard. The mixer will appear in one of three possible configurations. But let's start with the Fader or Basic view, shown in Figure 6.4.

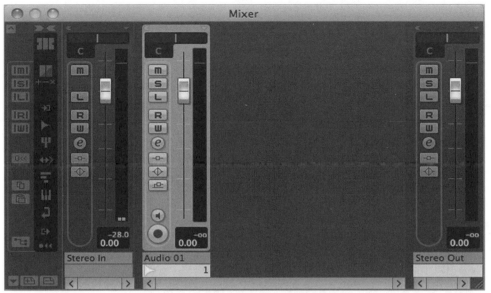

Figure 6.4: The Fader or Basic Mixer view

If your Mixer looks taller than the one in Figure 6.4, click the Hide buttons (shown in Figure 6.5) at the far left border of the Mixer to hide the Routing and/or Extended view. The Mixer allows you to see and adjust all the Faders of all channels from a centralized window while you're listening to some or all of the tracks.

You'll also notice the View controls on the left-hand side of the Mixer. Each of those small icons represents the track types. Clicking the icon will show (gray) or hide (orange) the associated tracks. For example, in Figure 6.4 we can see the Input Channel Fader. But that's a track we won't be using during mixing, so click the Show/Hide Input Channels button to remove that track type from view. This allows you to keep your Mixer organized and only show you the track types you'll need for mixing.

Each Mixer channel has its own Edit button. This allows you to access the VST Channel Settings window for any track.

The Extended Mixer View

When you click the Show/Hide Extended View button, the Mixer will double in height, as shown in Figure 6.5.

The Extended Mixer View can display a variety of different controls. In Figure 6.5, the first of two EQ views is being displayed. But you can choose a different set of controls by clicking the icons in the Extended View controller. Figure 6.6 shows what each of these buttons will display.

We won't be going over all of these different controls. But we will be using the Inserts, Equalizers, and Meters in this chapter. (We'll

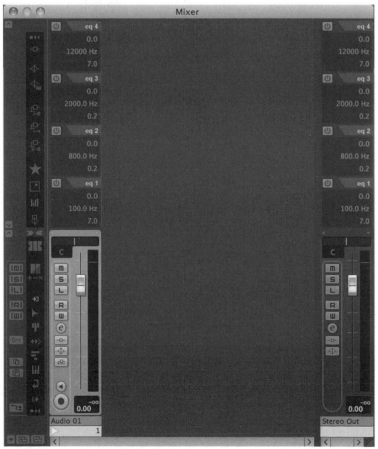

Figure 6.5: The Extended Mixer View

Figure 6.6: Extended View
controller options

learn about Sends in chapter 7.) Clicking on the Inserts icon will populate the Extended Mixer View with the eight Insert slots, and it will do that across all Mixer channels. The same is true of clicking any of the Extended View controllers: it applies the controls across the entire Mixer. However, if you'd like specific controls on one track, you can click on the Channel Extended View dropdown box (see Figure 6.6), and choose which controls you'd like to see on a channel-by-channel basis.

The Routing Mixer View

At the top of the Mixer, there is one more Mixer view we can reveal. Click the Show Routing View button (see Figure 6.5), and then refer to Figure 6.7 to see the controls.

Figure 6.7: The Routing Mixer View

At the top of the Routing View, you will find the input and output settings for each track. These are identical to the input and output settings on the Inspector of the Project window. Underneath, you'll find a reverse phase switch that can be enabled if you need to correct for phase cancellation. (Two tracks out of phase will cancel each other out.) There's also an Input Gain knob that allows you to increase or decrease the signal from the track as it enters the channel. This is another reason why recording in 32-bit is important, because you can dramatically increase the signal without clipping the audio engine of Cubase. To adjust the knob, you must hold the Shift button on your computer keyboard while turning the knob with your mouse. Alternately, you can double-click the numeric display and type in the desired increase or decrease. For values below the default of 0.0 dB, you must enter a "-" followed by the integers.

Going Big with the Mixer View

Even though the Mixer has customizable width and height, I prefer to leave it with all three views (Faders, Extended, and Routing) visible at all times and as wide as the computer monitor display will allow. If I'm using a computer with two monitor displays, I can keep the Project window and Mixer visible simultaneously. An example of this is shown in Figure 6.8. The monitor that displays the Mixer has enough room left at the bottom that it can also display the control panels of assorted VST plug-ins.

Figure 6.8: Project Window and Mixer on two 1920 X 1200 displays

If I'm using a laptop with only its built-in monitor display, I can quickly recall or close the Mixer by typing F3, or use the VST Channel Settings or the Inspector to make Mixer adjustments on an individual channel basis.

Track Order and Appearance in the Mixer

In the Track column of the Project window, you may have noticed that all the tracks are numbered from top to bottom. That numbering is identical to the left-to-right track order in the Mixer. For example, in Figure 6.9, we see one MIDI, Instrument, and Audio track.

Figure 6.9: Track Column and corresponding Mixer channels

Since the MIDI track is first in the Track Column, it is numbered 1 and is the left-most track in the Mixer. The Instrument and MIDI tracks 2 and 3 follow down the Track Column and across the Mixer. Therefore, when you rearrange the tracks in the Track Column, both their numbering and placement in the Mixer will be adjusted accordingly.

Track Types and the Extended Mixer View

It's important to recognize that different track types will offer different options in the Extended Mixer View. For example, the Mixer in Figure 6.9 has one MIDI, one Instrument, and one Audio track. The Show Inserts button (see Figure 6.6) has been clicked so that the Extended Mixer View is currently displaying Inserts across all three tracks. But if you look closely, the Inserts look different on the MIDI track compared to the Instrument and Audio tracks. That's because MIDI tracks don't make sound, but there are MIDI-specific Inserts you can use (such as arpeggiators and the Beat Designer) to modify the MIDI data in real-time. However, MIDI Inserts are quite different from the Audio Inserts used on Instrument and Audio tracks. Audio Inserts actually process the audio generated by the track in real-time. Basically, MIDI tracks don't have certain Mixer controls such as Audio Inserts, EQ, or Sends to FX Channels. For example, if the Equalizers button were pressed (see Figure 6.6), EQ controls would appear on the Extended Mixer View for the Instrument and Audio tracks, but the MIDI track would still display MIDI Inserts.

You may have also noticed that the Fader of MIDI tracks is turned all the way down by default. (See Figure 6.9.) It may seem counterproductive to turn a newly created track all the way down before you've even used it. But there's an important reason for this. Since a MIDI Fader is actually transmitting MIDI continuous controller 7 (volume), any default setting might adversely affect the loudness of that sound coming from either a VST Instrument or an external MIDI synthesizer (or other sound-generating device). Therefore, a MIDI Fader is designed to transmit nothing upon its creation, which is why it's turned all the way down. Then if you determine that the track volume needs to be adjusted, you can move the Fader accordingly.

The Cubase Signal Flow

After you've made Instrument or audio recordings, it's important to understand the journey that audio signal takes through Cubase. That journey is known as signal flow. Signal flow is a lot like a road map, which, when used properly, can help you arrive at your desired destination. The same is true for the destinations of your tracks, because if you don't know the signal flow, the sound from your tracks can easily get lost. In a tape-based studio, it was easier to see the signal flow, because you could just trace the wires leading from one audio component to another. (The Mixer in Cubase makes this process even less transparent, because DAW software has no cables.) But once it hit the Mixer, you had to know how the signal flowed through it to determine the destination of the audio.

Classic Mixer Signal Flow

Based on tried-and-true methodology, the producers, engineers, and mixer-designers developed a signal flow that would deliver consistent and predictable audio results: Input > Inserts > EQ > Prefader Sends > Fader. (The Cubase Sends are usually postfader and used for effects such as reverb and delay. We'll explore Sends in the next chapter.) This is known as the classic signal flow, and most contemporary mixers use this to move audio from one point to another. It is the signal flow used by Cubase.

Signal Flow of the VST Channel Settings Window

Click the Edit button (see Figure 6.4) on any Instrument or Audio track to reveal the VST Channel Settings window. Now let's explore the classic signal flow as shown in Figure 6.10.

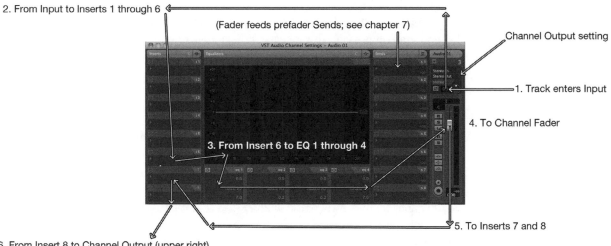

Figure 6.10: Classic signal flow of the VST Channel Settings window

I know this looks like a very roundabout signal flow. However, there is a method to the madness. First, the signal from the track enters channel Input. Second, the signal flows to Inserts 1 through 6. You'll notice that 1 through 6 are labeled i1 through i6 with light blue lettering. (You may be confused as to why the signal doesn't proceed through Inserts 7 and 8 [i7 and i8 in orange lettering]. That's because they are postfader Inserts, meaning that they are fed after the signal passes through the Fader.) Third, the signal flows through the four EQs. Fourth, the signal is passed from the last EQ to the Channel Fader. Fifth, the signal from the Fader is sent to both the Sends (see chapter 7) and Inserts

7 and 8. Sixth, the signal from Insert 8 travels to the channel Output destination in the upper right-hand corner of the VST Channel Settings window. In this case, it travels to the Stereo Output, which is controlled by the Master Fader. We'll discuss the Master Fader more in chapters 7 and 8.

Signal Flow in the Mixer

Now that you know how the signal flows through the VST Channel Settings window, it's easy to relate it to the Mixer. If you look closely at the Routing View (Figure 6.7) and the Extended View Controllers (Figures 6.6 and 6.7), all of the VST Channel Settings are duplicated there. But instead of flowing (mostly) left to right, they flow from top to bottom. The Sends* and Inserts 7 and 8, however, are still fed by the Fader output.

The Method and Madness of the Classic Signal Flow

When you start mixing, you'll start applying the three actions we discussed earlier: loudness, direction, and focus. But let's discuss why the signal flows the way it does.

Inserts

After signal leaves the channel inputs, it flows into the Inserts. The Insert slots are empty by default; into them you can install VST effect plug-ins. Inserts are very similar to guitar pedals, in that the signal flows from one pedal into the next. Also, the processed sound travels from one Insert to the other. Therefore, the types of plug-ins you can use on Inserts are generally any volume-oriented effect. Plug-ins such as compressors, de-essers, expanders, noise gates, and EQs will function properly when assigned to Inserts rather than Sends. (See chapter 7, "Plug-in Effects on Inserts and Sends.")

But the order in which the effects are assigned has a lot to do with how they'll interact with one another in the signal flow. For example, let's say you install an EQ plug-in first, followed by a compressor. In this case, any changes you make to the EQ will alter the response of the compressor. That's usually not a desirable situation. Instead, EQs should come after compressors, which is the reason that the Inserts come before the Cubase EQ. We'll learn more about using Inserts in chapter 7.

EQ

After the signal passes through Insert 6 (or the last populated Insert slot), the signal flows into the EQ. As I mentioned before, EQ allows you to focus on certain frequencies to be emphasized or deemphasized. But why not place the EQ after the Fader? You could certainly do this by adding a separate EQ plug-in into Inserts 7 or 8. But it's better to have the Fader be in control of the loudness, so that it has the final determination of the channel volume. Plus, if the Cubase EQ came after the Fader, the Sends (see chapter 7) would not receive the same tonally focused signal. And since the Fader is available to you in so many places, it's easy to adjust.

Channel Fader and Pan Control

These are the most essential controls for mixing. They each operate on the channel in its entirety, meaning that all of the processing that happens with Inserts and EQ is going to arrive at the Fader and the Pan control. (See Figure 6.2.) This gives them the "final say" as to how loud or soft the channel is (loudness) as well as in which ear (direction) the listener will be able to hear most, if not all, of the signal.

---

* Sends can be configured for pre- or postfader operation.

Getting into the Mix

Now that we know about the Cubase Mixer, its settings and signal flow, and the three actions of mixing, let's start applying what we've learned. For the rest of this section, go ahead and load the "The Right Track Matt R07.cpr" project from the disc that came with this book. (See appendix A, "Using the Included Disc.") The project contains several MIDI, Instrument, and Audio tracks and is in desperate need of mixing. Therefore, get ready to apply the three actions of mixing.

Taking a Listen

This is a fairly simple project with only nine audible tracks, but it will still present you with some challenges. Some will be easier to solve than others. Go ahead and take a listen to the R07 version. You'll notice that we can hear plenty of drums, bass, tambourine, and the synth pad (Comp Pad), but the vocals are a little buried, and the acoustic guitar (Q-Stick) is only clearly audible when it's being played loudly. We've got some work to do.

Creating a Group Channel Track

Notice that there are three drum tracks: Kick, Snare, and Hats. This is because the original drum track (SR Alta Kit) was separated into separate channels using the Dissolve Part command. That makes it really easy to adjust the loudness, direction, and focus of each individual drum sound.

However, it also means that if we find ourselves needing to adjust the volume of all the drums equally, we'll have to move three separate Faders rather than one. Plus, if we wanted to apply an Insert plug-in or EQ the entire drum set, we'd have to make identical adjustments to three different tracks. Fortunately, we can make all of those tasks easier by creating a Group Channel track. Click the Project menu, select Add Track, and then select Group Channel. A dialog box will ask you how many Group Channels you'd like and in what configuration. For our purposes, create two stereo Group Channels. (Only in rare occasions would you want to create mono Group Channels.) The Group Channels are added to the bottom of the Track Column and appear at the far right of the Mixer, as shown in Figure 6.11.

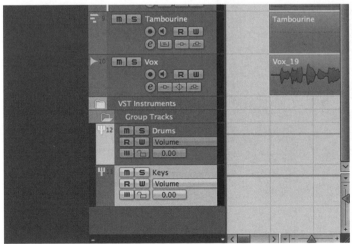
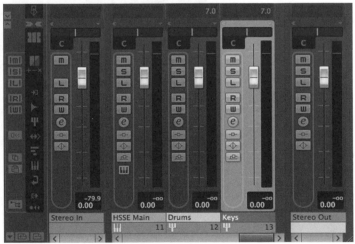

Figure 6.11: Group Channels in the Project window and Mixer, names changed

You can double-click on either the Project window or Mixer to change each Group Channel name. Change Group 1 to Drums and Group 2 to Keys. (See Figure 6.11.) Then type and hold the Shift key on your computer keyboard, and click on the first and last of the three Drum channels in the Mixer, as shown in Figure 6.12.

Figure 6.12: Selecting the three Drum channels (Extended Mixer View removed for clarity)

All three channels are now a light gray, indicating that they've been selected. Now before you lift off the Shift key (if you already have, hold it down again), click on the audio Output setting of any selected track, as shown in Figure 6.13.

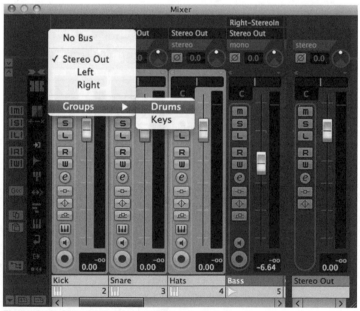

Figure 6.13: Channel Output settings

Normally a channel's Output is assigned to the Stereo Out by default, meaning that the signal will flow to the Master Fader. (See chapter 8.) But now we can interrupt that signal flow and send the signal from all three Drum channels into the Drums group. Doing so will make it possible to adjust the overall volume of all three tracks, simply by adjusting the Drums Group Channel Fader. (The Channel Faders won't move when you adjust the Group Fader, but the volume will adjust based on the position of the Group Fader.)

You might think that since we created a Keys Group, we can repeat this process for the Comp Pad and Rhodes channels. Don't do this quite yet, because we'll need to discuss how to add output channels to VST Instruments in a moment.

Applying the "Big Three" Mixing Actions

Now we're going to really start mixing this project by applying the "Big Three" actions of volume, pan, and EQ. But before we do, I think it's important to stress that mixing has a lot to do with personal taste. There can be tens or even hundreds of different iterations of a mix, and all of them can be good for different reasons. For example, when Prince mixes a song, he usually does several different versions, only one of which makes it to the CD or MP3 release. One producer would mix a song one way, while ten others would mix it ten different ways, and they might all sound wonderful for different reasons. With that in mind, you can use the mix settings I'm about to describe, but don't be afraid to go with what your ears are telling you to do. Everyone's ears are different, but we can still create a mix that meets the expectations of the client, the listener, and you.

Adjusting Loudness with Channel Faders

Adjusting volume is done by clicking and dragging the Channel Faders. We already know the drums are a little loud, so I'm going to reduce the volume of the Drums group to –5.5. When I do, the Bass channel is a little loud, so I'll turn that down to –6.5. Both of those Fader moves have helped the vocals become more present in the mix. However, the Comp Pad and Rhodes channels are too loud. Both of those channels (including the Tambourine channel) are coming from the same VST Instrument (HALion Sonic SE) on separate MIDI channels. Right now, all of the audio coming out of that VST Instrument is being premixed together by HALion Sonic SE (hereby known as HSSE) and delivered to the Mixer on the HSSE Main channel. We could adjust the corresponding MIDI Channel Faders, but it would be better if we had full mixing capabilities of all three HSSE sounds. To do that, we'll need to activate more output channels for HSSE.

Activating More VST Instrument Output Channels

Every VST Instrument has a different numbers of discrete audio outputs. In the case of HSSE, there are up to sixteen stereo output channels. But by default, only one is activated when the plug-in is added to the VST Instrument rack. To activate more output channels, you'll need to click the Devices menu and select VST Instruments, or just type F11 on your computer keyboard. The VST Instruments rack and the Output Activate button are shown in Figure 6.14.

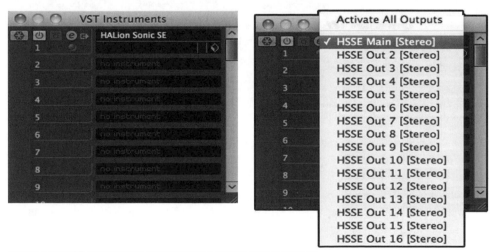

Figure 6.14: VST Instruments rack/Output Activate button clicked

You can see that at the top of the Activate Output menu, there's an option for Activate All Outputs. You could select that, but the result would be fifteen additional HSSE channels added to the Mixer. This is why only one stereo pair is activated by default. Otherwise, you can really fill up the Mixer by adding a lot of outputs. Since we only need three, let's activate HSSE Out 2 (Stereo) and HSSE Out 3 (Stereo). HSSE Main (Stereo) was already activated by default, indicated by the check to the left of the output name. Now when you look at the Mixer, you will see the newly activated VST Instrument outputs, as shown in Figure 6.15.

Figure 6.15: Newly activated VST Instruments output channels

Now click the Edit button on the first VST Instrument Rack slot (see Figure 6.14) to reveal the HSSE control panel, as shown in Figure 6.16.

Figure 6.16: HSSE control panel, mix tab, and output assignments

The Comp Syn, Rhodes, and Tambourine sounds are on parts 1, 2, and 3, respectively. Click on the Mix tab at the top to reveal the Output column at the far right side of the control panel. Set the second part to Out 2 and the third part to Out 3. Then close the HSSE control panel and the VST Instruments Rack, and locate the newly activated channels on the mixer. Now is a good time to route all three channels into the Keys Group we created earlier. See "Creating a Group Channel Track" earlier in this chapter.

Next, turn the new channels down to –6.0, –3.5, and –2, respectively. (If you'd like to rename the new channels, double-click on their names and enter the desired text.) Now we're starting to hear a better mix with more balanced volumes.

Adjusting Direction with the Pan Controls

Since we haven't adjusted any Pan controls, the mix is sounding decidedly monophonic. Certain sounds, such as the drums and keyboard, already have a little stereo direction, because they've been programmed that way. But individual instruments and tracks are hard to pick out in the mix. Therefore, it's time to start adding some direction with Pan.

I want the guitar channel (Q-Stick) to have a strong presence in this mix, but it's getting lost in the center position. So try adjusting the Pan control (see Figure 6.2) to R25. It should suddenly become much easier to hear. Now since we moved the guitar to the right, let's move the keyboard channels (HSSE Main and HSSE Out 2) to the left at about L50. This will help the instruments in the center position (most notably the vocals) be more easily heard. But the tambourine (HSSE Out 3) is also center, so try pushing it to the left at about L75. Even though we've panned the keyboard sound to the left, the tambourine is clearer when it's on the opposite side of the hi-hats of the drum set. Those are usually panned to the right for a right-handed drummer with audience-perspective panning.

Adjusting Focus with EQ

Now that the Vocal channel (Vox) has been made more present by the Fader and Pan adjustments to the other channels, we need to craft some EQ to help bring it out of the mix. It's probably loud enough, but it sounds a little boxy and muddy. Click the Edit button on the Vox channel to open the VST Channel Settings window, as shown in Figure 6.17.

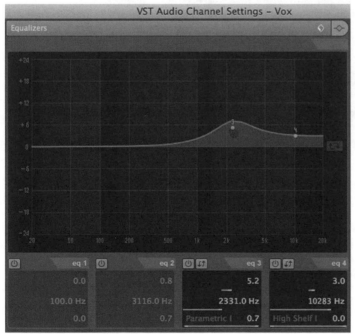

Figure 6.17: VST Channel Settings window of Vox channel with adjusted EQ focus

EQ1 and EQ2 are still powered off, as indicated by their power buttons. Since this vocal recording doesn't have a lot of low or low-mid frequencies, they can remain off, as they are the EQs that normally focus those frequencies. However, EQ3 focuses high-mid frequencies, and some focus here will help immensely. EQ3 has been powered up, which made the small dot with a "3" on the EQ line visible. I dragged that little dot upward until I liked the sound. If you'd rather type in the Gain, Frequency, and Q-Factor settings as they're shown in Figure 6.17, just double-click on each numeric value, and enter 5.2, 2331.0, and 0.7, respectively.

But after I added that high-mid focus, I felt as though putting a little shine on the high frequencies with EQ4 would help. See Figure 6.17 for the proper placement of the "4" dot, or enter the values using the same procedure as editing EQ3 in the last paragraph. Afterward, you'll notice the vocals have been made a bit shinier and more noticeable by the high-mid and high EQ focus.

Now let's listen to the Q-Stick Acoustic Guitar channel. It also sounds a little boxy, but it has a few other characteristics we can improve upon. Click the Q-Stick channel Edit button to reveal the VST Channel Settings window, as shown in Figure 6.18.

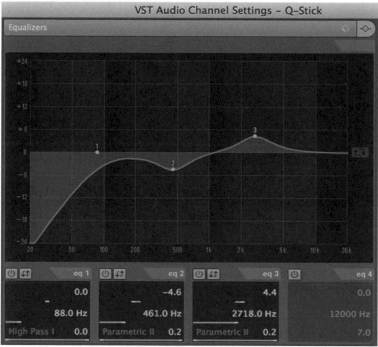

Figure 6.18: VST Channel Settings window of Q-Stick channel with adjusted EQ focus

I really wanted to hear more of the pick noise—that is, the sound of the pick as it comes across the strings—and it is found in the high-mid frequencies. Therefore, I edited EQ3 to focus more on those frequencies. But then the low-mids sounded a little throaty, so I used EQ2 to defocus the frequencies around 461.0 Hz. (Notice that the 2 dot has been moved below the EQ line, and the Gain value is a negative value of –4.6.) Lastly, there's some low-frequency thumping caused when the player's arm (my arm) bounced off the guitar body. To reduce that offending sound, I set the EQ1 Q-Factor to High Pass 1 and changed the frequency to 88 HZ. That means that any frequencies below 88 Hz will be dramatically reduced. A visualization of that is the steep drop of the left curve past the 1 dot for EQ1. Now when we listen to the guitar in context, we can hear it more clearly with plenty of pick noise. The volume of the guitar (and the vocal) is still somewhat inconsistent, but we'll fix that in the next chapter.

Mix On, d'Artagnan

Now that we've used the Big Three mixing actions of loudness, direction, and focus (or volume, pan, and EQ), our project has a much improved and balanced mix. If you'd like to listen to the results of this chapter, you can load the "The Right Track Matt R08.cpr" project from the disc that came with this book. (See appendix A, "Using the Included Disc.") But we still have a ways to go. We still need to add effects in the Inserts and Sends. But which effects and which plug-ins will we use? Proceed to chapter 7 to find out.

Chapter 7

EFFECTS: INSERTS, SENDS, AND FX CHANNELS

In the early days of audio recording, there were no electronic special effects (also known as effects or FX). If the engineer or producer decided that the recording should include reverb or other time-based or spatial effects, then the instrumentation had to be placed within a suitable acoustic environment during the recording. That way, the sound of the concert hall, recital room, or sound stage would become part of the recording. Later, engineers found ways to simulate acoustic environments by running microphones into separate acoustically suitable rooms and recording the sound of a speaker as it filled the room with the recorded tracks. Then came early reverbs based on plates or springs. Then electronic effects such as digital reverbs added wonderful spatial effects for the studios that could afford them. (Since I couldn't afford the Lexicon 224XL at $7,900, my first digital reverb was the $950 Yamaha SPX90.) Today, Cubase comes with a variety of reverbs, including the fantastic REVerence convolution reverb. (Living in this era has spoiled us rotten.)

But the earliest effects were not special, per se. Rather, dynamic effects such as compressors and limiters helped tame and limit the dynamic range of acoustic instrument recordings. For example, the human voice can go from a whisper to a roar, making it possible for the recording to become either too soft or too loud. Early compressors were based on tubes, transistors, and even optical sensors. Today, the compressors (and the other dynamic processors) that come with DAW software are digital and offer precise control of the dynamics of the recorded tracks. Before proceeding, make sure that you've read chapter 6 to understand the concepts of signal flow, Inserts, and Sends. In this chapter, you will learn:

- The differences between Inserts and Sends.
- How to properly use the signal flow through the Inserts.
- How to use some of the most common effects.
- The concept of the FX Channel track.

The Concept and History of Plug-ins

In 1996, Steinberg (the creator of Cubase) created a plug-in technology called VST, or Virtual Studio Technology. The concept of plug-ins was not new. Other creative software programs (such as the photo-editing program Photoshop from Adobe) had plug-in capabilities. Plug-ins are specialized software programs that plug into and expand upon the capabilities of the host program.

What was new about VST was that it defined a standard upon which anyone (even you) could write his or her own plug-ins. And since Steinberg provided the VST Software Developers Kit (SDK) for free, no one needed to pay Steinberg to create and market a plug-in. The result was a firestorm of development that continues to this day, and we are all the beneficiaries of a wealth of incredible plug-ins that either come with or can be purchased for use in Cubase.

All of the real-time effects in Cubase are based on plug-ins. It is that real-time capability that is the most profound advantage of VST plug-ins. By tapping into the processing power of your computer's CPU (Central Processing Unit), all of the effects or instrument plug-ins can be applied instantly. This makes them behave just like hardware processors such as rack-mounted compressors and reverbs. Prior to VST plug-ins, those types of effects had to be rendered (processed offline) onto the audio file. That took time and tried the patience of many an artist, engineer, and producer. Plus, if you didn't like the result, you had to undo and render the effect all over again. The advantages of VST plug-ins, both in terms of price and creative freedom, are clear. (Did I mention we're spoiled rotten?)

Effect and Plug-in Placement and Classification

Studios used to have only a few varieties of effects—usually compressors, delays, perhaps a modulation effect such as a flanger or chorus, and a reverb. Guitarists have always had a plethora of stomp-boxes including distortion, phaser, and wah-wah effects. But today, there are so many effect plug-ins that come with Cubase that they've been organized into different classifications. For the rest of this chapter, go ahead and load the "The Right Track Matt R08.cpr" project from the disc that came with this book. (See appendix A, "Using the Included Disc.")

The Differences Between Dry and Wet Signals

I know this sounds more like a weather forecast, but when you're using any effect (hardware or software), you have to understand the difference between dry and wet signals. Dry signal is the original unprocessed sound that remains uneffected as it passes through the plug-in. Wet signal is the processed sound after it passes to the output of the plug-in. Some effect classifications require that only wet (processed) signal appear at the plug-in output. But others require a mix of dry (unprocessed) and wet (processed) signals. To that end, you'll notice that some effect control panels include a mix or balance control with which to blend the wet and dry signal. As you will see in a moment, the presence of that mix control has a lot to do with whether the plug-in is used on an Insert or a Send.

Plug-in Effects on Inserts and Sends

There are very few rules in recording that you cannot break. However, determining the proper placement of plug-ins into the signal flow, either on the Inserts or Sends, is paramount for the effect to function properly. Therefore, here are a few guidelines that will help you make the initial determination.

- Plug-ins that alter the volume (such as compressors, limiters, and gates) should go on an Insert.
- Plug-ins that provide spatial effects should be used with a combination of Sends and FX Channel tracks.

- If the control panel of the plug-in has a mix or balance control, it might work best when used with a combination of Sends and FX Channel tracks.
- If the plug-in has a mix control and is being used on a Send, the control must be set to 100 percent wet.

Examples of Insert Effects

For guitarists or any other musicians that use stomp-boxes or guitar pedals, the Inserts are very easy to understand. By referring to Figure 6.10 in the previous chapter, you can see that signal flows from Insert slot 1 through slot 6. This is identical to stomp-boxes, in that the sound from the first pedal flows into the next, to the next, and so on. An example of this can be seen in Figure 7.1.

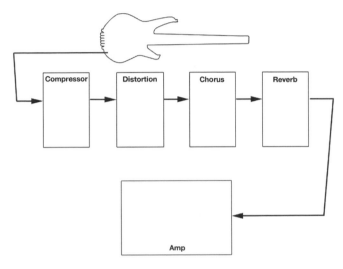

Figure 7.1: Signal flow of guitar stomp-boxes

All of the stomp-boxes pictured in Figure 7.1 are types of effects you will find in Cubase. Let's see how the effects are listed in Cubase. Click the Edit button on the Q-Stick channel to reveal the VST Channel Settings window as shown in Figure 7.2, then click the first Insert slot (i1) to reveal the plug-in list. (Figure 7.2 is shown with slot 2 selected.)

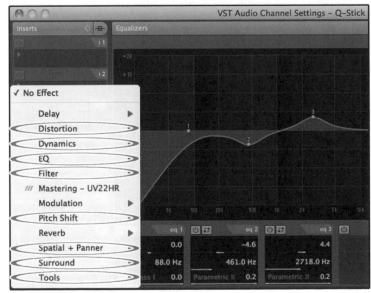

Figure 7.2: Plug-in list

I've circled all of the effect categories that work best as Inserts. None of the effects in these categories will have a mix control, so any sound present at the input will be processed and sent to the output without any of the dry (original) signal. (You'll notice that the Mastering—UV22HR is not circled. This must be used on an Insert but is a very specialized plug-in that we will discuss in the next chapter.)

Modulation Effects

In Figure 7.2, you'll notice that Modulation is not circled. That's because modulation effects can be used either as Inserts or as Sends. Most of the modulation plug-in control panels will have a mix control like the ones found on the StudioChorus, shown in Figure 7.3.

Figure 7.3: StudioChorus plug-in left and right mix controls

The presence of a mix control on any plug-in control panel means that it can be used on an Insert or a Send. If used on an Insert, the mix control would be adjusted somewhere between wet and dry. However, if it's being used on a Send, the mix control must be 100 percent wet. That's because the dry signal will come from the track itself, and the wet signal will come through the FX Channel track, which we'll discuss in a moment.

Examples of Send Effects

If you look at the plug-in list in Figure 7.2, you'll see that Delay, Modulation, and Reverb are not circled. These plug-ins also have mix controls, which means they will work on Inserts. But delay and reverb effects work best when used as Sends. This is because Sends allow you to share the plug-in processing among several tracks. This provides the advantage of putting multiple tracks through one effect, which makes them sound complementary. You also only need to use one plug-in to process several if not all tracks, which saves on computer processing power. Many new DAW users are under the impression that for every track that needs reverb, they must apply a separate reverb. But by using Sends and FX Channel tracks, all of the tracks can be processed using only one plug-in.

Reverbs, delays, and most modulation plug-ins are time-based effects. In other words, they all have some sort of time control. Modulation effects have times in the milliseconds, where delays and reverbs can offer multiple seconds of time.

Assigning Plug-ins to Inserts

Now that we know what kinds of effects work best on Inserts, we can start to apply some to our song. Let's start with the Q-Stick channel. Click that channel's Edit button (see Figure 6.4) to reveal the VST Channel Settings window, then click the Solo button so that we're only hearing that track. Now start playback and listen to the guitar. You'll notice that at the end of measures 4 and 12, there are some very loud 16th note strums. The rest of the track has a pretty balanced dynamic range. So let's use a dynamic plug-in to tame the loudness of this track.

Assigning a Compressor to the Q-Stick Channel

A compressor is one of the most useful tools for dynamic control, and the Q-Stick channel is a perfect example of a track that needs some compression. It's useful to have playback engaged while making the following settings, so that you can hear the difference as you go. Click on the first Insert slot (i1), select Dynamics (see Figure 7.2), then select Compressor from the plug-in list. The Compressor plug-in control panel will appear. At the top of the control panel, click the Preset field (see Figure 7.4), which then displays a Preset list. Double-click the Strummed Acoustic Guitar preset from the list. The control panel should now be loaded with the settings shown in Figure 7.4.

Figure 7.4: The Compressor control panel and Preset settings

Don't be confused by the preset name. I know it sounds like we might be calling up a guitar sound for a VST Instrument. But instead, we're calling up preset values for all of the Compressor controls. If you're still listening to playback, you'll notice that the track doesn't have as wide a dynamic range.

A Primer on Compressors

What the Compressor is doing is reducing the loudness (as indicated in the GR or gain reduction meter) during the loud spots. The Threshold control is set at –19.1 dB, which means that any sound louder than –19.1 dB will be compressed. The Ratio control of 2.18 means that every time the Threshold is exceeded by 2.18 dB, only 1 dB of volume will be added to the signal. So if we exceeded the Threshold by 6.54 dB, only 3 dB of volume will be added.

But if the volume is being reduced, why does the track sound louder? That's because the Make-Up control is set to Auto, which means that the plug-in is monitoring how much gain is being reduced, and increasing the output of the plug-in accordingly to make up for it. If the result was too much gain reduction, you could disable the Auto button and set the Make-Up knob manually.

Auditioning the "Before and After"

Hardware processors have bypass buttons that allow you to hear the dry versus wet signal for a "before and after" comparison. You can do the same thing using the Bypass button on the plug-in control panel (see Figure 7.4) or by using the Bypass button on the Insert slot, as shown in Figure 7.5.

When the Bypass button is gray, you can hear the processing of the plug-in. When the Bypass button is yellow, the wet signal is removed, leaving only the dry, unprocessed signal.

Figure 7.5: Insert slot Bypass button, currently engaged

Recalling the Plug-in Control Panel

The Insert Slot Bypass buttons only appear when they have plugs-in assigned to them. The same is true of the Edit button. (See Figure 7.5.) If you've closed a plug-in control panel, you can reveal it by clicking the Edit button.

Assigning a Compressor to the Vox Channel

Repeat the process of assigning the Compressor, but this time do so on the Vox track. When you listen to the project, the vocals have started overpowering the rest of the tracks. But they're not constantly overpowering, so the Compressor will be very useful. Click on the Preset window of the Compressor plug-in you just added to the Vox channel, and select the Hard Rock Vocals preset, as shown in Figure 7.6.

Figure 7.6: The Compressor with Hard Rock Vocals preset (modified)

Make sure the channel isn't soloed, so that you can hear the Compressor in context with the other tracks. You'll notice that the Vox channel has become louder, so this is a case in which the auto Make-Up must be disabled and the Make-Up control set manually. I found that 3.0 dB seemed to tame the loudness quite effectively, but your mileage may vary. I also disabled the Live setting, which allows the Compressor to "look ahead" at the upcoming signal. This makes the transitions between signal below and above the Threshold smoother.

Assigning a Chorus to the Bass Channel

Now that we know how to assign plug-ins to an Insert, let's add a chorus effect to the Bass channel. A light amount of chorus can add spatial depth to any instrument, but the effect is more obvious when the track is monophonic to begin with. That's why we're going to use the Bass track for this example. It's not in dire need of an effect, but a little chorus will add a nice finishing touch. Repeat the process outlined in "Assigning a Compressor to the Q-Stick Channel," but this time use the Bass channel, and select Chorus from the Modulation category (see Figure 7.2) in the plug-in list. Then click the Preset window from the Chorus control panel, and select the Flying Bass preset, as shown in Figure 7.7.

Figure 7.7: Chorus with the Flying Bass preset

The Chorus does not add a profound effect, rather a very subtle pitch modulation mixed with the original dry signal. The Flying Bass preset adds only a small amount of effect and retains the low end of the bass guitar. That's because the low filter is set to 495 Hz, which means that the bass frequencies below the point will be unaffected by the Chorus and therefore maintain the rich low end. If you want a more pronounced effect, you could increase either the Rate or Width controls. Since the Chorus plug-in is used on an Insert, the Mix knob is set in the middle at 58 percent, indicating a balance of 42 percent dry and 58 percent wet.

Reordering the Inserts

Now that we have a Chorus in Insert slot 1 of the Bass channel, we might feel the need to add Compressor to the signal flow. However, all compressors should usually come before any spatial effects. Fortunately, Cubase has a very easy way to modify the order of the Inserts. You can do it from any screen that shows all the Channel Inserts (i.e., Insert slots in the Inspector, VST Channel Settings window, or Extended Mixer View). When you hover your mouse over the slot number (i1, i2, i3, etc.), the pointer will turn into a hand. Click and drag the slot number to the desired empty slot, as shown in Figure 7.8.

When you release the mouse button, the Chorus will now appear in slot i2, leaving you to assign the Compressor into slot i1. I chose the Rock Bass Compression preset, but the Auto setting pulled too much volume away. So I disabled Auto and set the Make-Up to 9.0 dB, as shown in Figure 7.9.

Figure 7.8: Reordering slot i1 to i2

Figure 7.9: Rock Bass Compression preset (modified) on the Bass channel

Reordering and Copying Inserts in the Extended Mixer View

When you are in the Extended Mixer View with Inserts showing (see "The Extended Mixer View" in chapter 6), you can click and drag Insert plug-ins to the slots of other like channels. In other words, you can drag MIDI Inserts to other MIDI or Instrument channels, or Audio Inserts to other Audio, Instrument, or Group channels. This process is shown in Figure 7.10.

 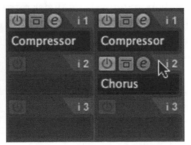

Figure 7.10: Dragging and moving an Insert plug-in to a different channel

If you'd rather duplicate the plug-in and its settings to another channel, hold the Alt/Option key on your computer keyboard at any time during the drag and prior to releasing the mouse button. You'll notice a small "+" sign under the mouse that indicates that you are making a copy. When you release the mouse button, the plug-in will be present on both channels, as shown in Figure 7.11.

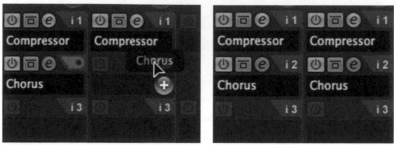

Figure 7.11: Dragging and copying an Insert plug-in to another channel

Now both channels will have their own discrete Chorus effects with identical settings. Altering the settings of one copied plug-in will have no affect on the plug-in from which it was copied. Personally, I didn't like the Chorus on the Q-Stick channel, because it made the guitar sound too processed and unnatural. So I clicked on the Chorus slot and chose No Effect to remove the plug-in.

Using Sends and FX Channel Tracks

As I've previously mentioned, time-based effects such as reverb and delay work best when assigned to Sends and FX Channel tracks. This allows several channels to share one plug-in, and also saves on computer processing power. For this example, we're going to add a reverb and delay effect to our project by adding FX Channel tracks. Then we'll be able to use the Sends to add those effects across multiple channels.

Creating an FX Channel Track

FX Channel tracks are added to the Project and Mixer windows. They are similar to Audio, Instrument, and Group Channel tracks, because they process audio signals. However, FX Channel tracks do not carry the signals of tracks or files. Instead, they are specialized tracks that return the signals from plug-ins back into the signal flow of the Mixer. Click the Project menu, select Add Track, and select FX Channel. The Add FX Channel Track dialog box will appear, as shown in Figure 7.12.

Figure 7.12: The Add FX Channel Track dialog box

The default configuration is Stereo. Only under rare circumstances would you ever use a mono configuration for an FX Channel track. Now click on the effect drop-down box, select the Reverb category, and select REVerence. When you click the Add Track button on the lower right of the dialog box, the REVerence control panel will appear, as shown in Figure 7.13.

Figure 7.13: The REVerence control panel

Click the Preset field, and choose the Music Academy preset. This is a very gentle reverb without a lot of decay, so it will work well on our mid-tempo project. Notice also that the default mix is set to 100 percent. This setting is critical when using any effect on an FX Channel track. For now, close the REVerence control panel, and take a look at both the Project window and Mixer. You'll notice that FX Channels have been added to the Track Column and Mixer respectively, as shown in Figure 7.14.

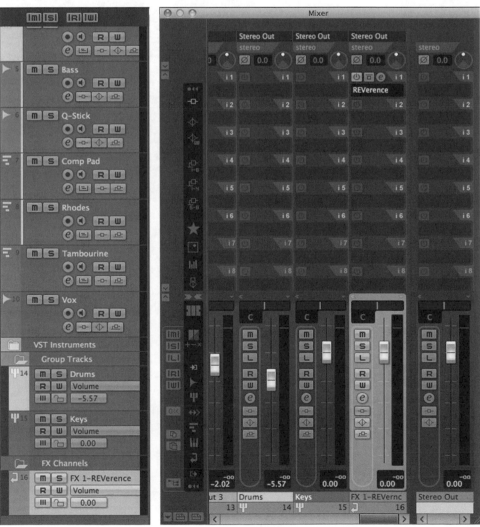

Figure 7.14: FX Channel track in the Track Column and Mixer

Notice that in the Extended Mixer View with Inserts showing, the REVerence reverb plug-in we just added is on Insert slot i1. The FX Channel itself looks very similar to any other channel. It even has Inserts, EQ, and Sends of its own. But instead of routing tracks to the channel, its sole purpose is to route the output of the inserted plug-in into the Mixer. But how do we get signal into the REVerence? We do that with the Sends of other channels.

Assigning Sends to FX Channel Tracks

Let's start by assigning the REVerence Reverb we just made to the Vox (vocal) channel. You can do this by selecting the Vox track in the Track Column, the VST Channel Settings window, or the Mixer in Extended Mixer View with Sends 1 to 8 showing. (See Figure 6.6 from the previous chapter.) I prefer to use the latter method, because this allows me to see all of the Sends on all of the tracks simultaneously. Now click on Send slot S1, and choose FX 1-REVerence, enable the Send power button, and adjust the Send fader, as shown in Figure 7.15.

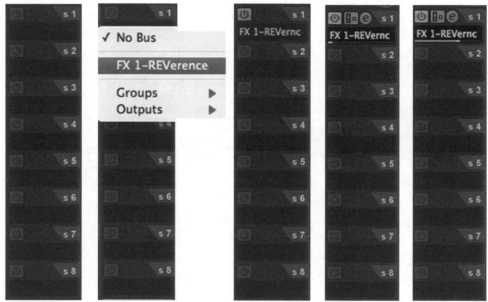

Figure 7.15: The channel Send assignment procedure

The Send Fader is a small, blue line that moves from left to right. By default, the Fader appears as a small dot at the far left of the slot. Click and drag that dot to send some signal from the Vox channel into the REVerence FX Channel track. The further you drag the Fader to the right, the more reverb you will hear on the vocals. If you need finer control, you can adjust the Fader either in the Sends tab of the Inspector or the VST Channel Settings window Sends. (See Figure 6.3 in the previous chapter.) Those methods have larger Send Faders and a numeric readout. The adjustment of the Fader is really a "season to taste" setting. I found that on this particular vocal track, a setting of –6 dB (or the approximate value shown in Figure 7.15) sounds about right.

If you'd like to customize any of the settings on the REVerence control panel, you'll notice that every Send that has an FX Channel track assigned to it has an Edit button. (See Figure 7.14.) Click on that button at any time to reveal the associated plug-in control panel.

Assigning and Adjusting Sends on Soloed Tracks

I make the following confusing mistake on a regular basis and want you to be aware of it. I sometimes have the Solo button enabled on the channel on which I want to use a Send *before* going through the procedure in Figure 7.15. But when I start adjusting the Send

Fader, I don't hear any effect being added to the signal. That's because the channel was soloed prior to turning on the Send power button, which results in the muting of all other channels, including the FX Channel. If this happens to you, just disable and reenable the channel Solo button on the channel on which you're adjusting the Send. Now that the power is enabled on the Send, the FX Channel track will also have its Solo enabled, which allows you to listen to the effect of the plug-in while you're adjusting the Send fader.

Assigning Other Channels to the FX Channel Track

Now you can repeat the procedure outlined in Figure 7.15 for any Instrument or Audio channel. To that end I'm going to add a little of the REVerence reverb to the Kick, Snare, and Q-Stick channels, as shown in Figure 7.16.

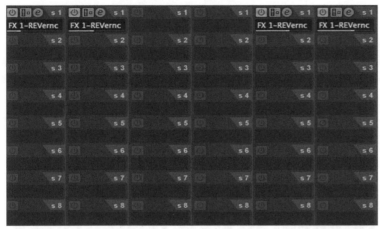

Figure 7.16: Multiple channels assigned to the FX 1-REVerence FX Channel track

You can see the advantages of doing this from the Extended Mixer View. We can assign and adjust the Sends and Faders across multiple channels. Notice that the Kick and Snare channels have lower Send Faders, while the Q-Stick and Vox channels have more. All of this is a "season to taste" setting decided upon by you and/or the client.

Creating Another FX Channel Track and Plug-in

Cubase is very flexible in its use of Sends and FX Channel tracks. You can create as many FX Channel tracks as you need, and you can assign any eight of those tracks to the eight sends of any channel. Let's explore this concept by creating a delay effect on another FX Channel track. Repeat the procedure described previously in "Creating an FX Channel Track." But when you see the Add FX Channel Track dialog box, choose the Delay category and the StereoDelay effect. Then choose the Alternating preset, and modify the settings as shown in Figure 7.17.

Figure 7.17: Modified settings for the Alternating preset, StereoDelay plug-in

Set the left and right Delay times to 1/8 and 1/4, respectively. Notice that the Sync buttons are enabled on the StereoDelay control panel. That will match the Delay settings to the tempo of the Cubase Project. Then turn the left Pan control to –100 (full left) and the right Pan control to 100 (full right). Notice that the Mix controls are both set to 100 percent wet, as is necessary with plug-ins on FX Channel tracks.

Now repeat the procedure described in "Assigning Sends to FX Channel Tracks," and do so on the Vox channel. But this time, assign Send slot 2 (S2) to the FX 2-StereoDelay FX Channel track. Now as you increase the Send Fader, you will hear some stereo delay (repeats bouncing from left to right) added to the vocals. I used a very low setting of –16 dB. Too high a setting, and it will sound as though you're mixing at the Grand Canyon. (Not that this would be a bad thing, as the scenery might inspire you.)

The Insert, EQ, and Sends Bypass Buttons

Figure 7.18: Inserts, EQ, and Sends Bypass buttons

There are multiple methods for bypassing an Insert, EQ, or Send. Since all of these devices have power buttons, you can simply turn off the power. Or for Inserts, you can use the Bypass buttons. But what if you wanted to disable all the devices at once? You may have already noticed the Insert, EQ, and Send Bypass buttons on the channels, as shown in Figure 7.18.

Clicking any of the Bypass buttons will disable all the Inserts, EQ bands, or Sends. When bypassed, the button will turn a pale yellow rather than the default colors that are shown in Figure 7.18. These buttons give you the ability to quickly audition the before and after sound of the corresponding plug-ins. Figure 7.18 depicts the buttons on a Mixer channel, but be aware that the same buttons can be found on the track in the Track Column.

Taking a Moment to Look (Listen) Back

If you want to hear my version of the mix, you can load the "The Right Track Matt R09.cpr" project from the disc that came with this book. (See appendix A, "Using the Included Disc.") But you should also load and listen to the project in its remixed state by loading "The Right Track Matt R07.cpr" project. This version had no mixing, EQ, or effects added. When you compare the R07 version to the R09 version, the difference is very noticeable. R07 sounds pretty flat and lifeless, while R09 sounds more open, balanced, and polished. When a project gets to point where you're happy with the mix, it's time to master it and share it with the world, which we'll do in the next chapter.

Chapter 8
MASTERING AND AUDIO MIXDOWN

Now that our project is sounding properly mixed, it's time to share it with the world by performing an Audio Mixdown. That process will create a stereo audio file, herein referred to as a "mixdown," and usually in WAV (Microsoft Wave Format), AIFF (Audio Interleaved File Format), or MP3 (MPEG-1 Layer 3) format. Once your Cubase Project has been exported, you can burn it to audio CD; publish it to your website, MySpace, or Facebook page; or make it available for purchase on iTunes or cdbaby.com, or any of a number of sites for distributing independent music. But Cubase has not only great mixing capabilities but also some really cool tools for audio mastering. I'm going to show you how to avail your projects of the mastering tools Cubase provides. In this chapter, I'm going to describe mastering in detail, but we'll also be discussing:

- The goals of mastering.
- My three-adjective approach to mastering.
- The Loudness War.
- Statistical analysis of various CD audio file examples.
- Audio mixdown of multiple audio file formats

The Dark Art of Mastering

Have you ever looked at the album credits and seen "Mastering by Bob Clearmountain" or "Mastering by Bob Ludwig"? Ever wonder what "mastering" is? The good news is that your name doesn't need to be Bob before you can master a mix, and that Cubase comes with great mastering tools. But that doesn't answer the question of what mastering is.

The Definition of Mastering

Because mastering is something of an ambiguous dark art, it has no easy definition. However, I've narrowed the long list down to the three basic goals of mastering:

1. Your last chance to add broad treatments to your mix.
2. Matching your mix to other commercial recordings in the same genre.
3. Matching all of your mixes prior to distribution as a collection.

Now let's explore what each of these goals mean in an audio context.

Broad Treatments

By now you should be really happy with the sound of each track within the project. However, when you listen to the mix of all those tracks, you will invariably determine that some overall improvements could be made. Are the overall bass frequencies of a project overbearing, or are they lacking? Is the overall volume of the project too low or too high? Does the mix of the project sound tinny or boxy, or does it lack definition? These are all questions that engineers are constantly analyzing during the mastering process.

But you'll notice that the questions are being asked of the project, not the individual tracks. This is a very important aspect of mastering. In other words, you may have applied individual EQ to the bass guitar and the bass drum to make each track sound tonally balanced. But now, how do those tracks sound when played together in the mix? The bottom line about this goal of mastering is that you're listening to the project as a whole rather than track by track. After listening to and analyzing the sound of the project, the mastering treatments you determine it needs are applied broadly to the entire mix.

Matching to Other Mixes of the Same Genre

In the world of rap and hip-hop, it's totally appropriate to lay in copious amounts of thunderous bass frequencies. However, it would probably be a mistake to apply the same mastering treatment to country or jazz projects. Similarly, jazz and orchestral projects have a much wider range of dynamics than heavy metal or punk projects. But who determines the appropriateness of any mastering treatment? Well, the artists, bands, producers, and mastering engineers certainly have a lot to do with it. But ultimately, it's the end-listener that has the final say. Basically, if you were mastering a project of a specific genre, it would behoove you to listen to a lot of commercial releases of music in the same genre.

Mastering Your Mixes as a Collection

If you produce nothing but singles, then you needn't worry about this aspect of mastering. But if you combine your own music or that of a client into a collection (CD, LP, Digipak, etc.), then making all the songs within that collection sound evenly balanced is critical. For example, the overall volumes of all the projects should be about the same. If they're not, the end-listener will be reaching for his or her volume control at the start of every song. Or if one song is much brighter (contains more high frequencies) than the others, the experience of listening to the album in its entirety would be disrupted. For example, if you were listening to Pink Floyd's *Dark Side of the Moon* and the song "Money" were noticeably quieter and contained more high frequencies than the rest of the songs, you'd certainly notice the difference. Essentially, if the song doesn't sound like the others on the record, you or the end-listener might just skip listening to the song. (Even though "Money," like the other songs, is expertly mixed and mastered, I usually skip it.) That's why all the songs in a collection need to have similar tonality and volume levels. Without that cohesion, the album will come across as a haphazardly slapped-together bunch of songs (like a "greatest hits" album of several bands) rather than a methodical approach that injects the signature sound of the band or artist on every song. Addressing the overall listening experience of the artist and end-listener alike is the most mature approach to mastering.

What to Expect from This Section

The size of this book will limit our ability to master a collection of songs. Therefore, I'm going to concentrate on the first two mastering goals: broad treatments and genre-matching.

Matt's Three-Adjective Approach to Mastering

I've mastered hundreds of songs for different clients. One of the first things I ask a client is, "How do you want the song (album, record, etc.) to sound?" Only on the rarest occasions do I get answers like, "Tame the high frequencies between 2.2 kHz and 6.6 kHz and make the average volume –10 dB below zero." Instead, they usually provide a list of general adjectives, such as, "Just make it punchy, shiny, and LOUD!" With those adjectives in mind, let's talk about the Cubase plug-ins that will produce what the client wants to hear.

Punchy Equals Compression

As we learned in the previous chapter, compression can decrease the dynamic range of an audio signal, thereby smoothing the loudness by minimizing the difference between loud and quiet passages. A fringe benefit of compression is that it can make the audio sound punchier. Cubase has a fantastic plug-in called the MultibandCompressor that applies different amounts of compression to different frequency bands.

Shiny Equals EQ

EQ, or tonal control, is a critical component of mastering. So when a client says "shiny," it usually means adding some high-mid or high frequencies, but can refer to the overall tonal clarity as well. Cubase comes with several different EQ plug-ins, or you can use the built-in 4-band EQ we've used on the Audio and Instrument tracks. As you'll see in a moment, the Master Fader has its own EQ, or you can choose a different EQ plug-in.

LOUD Equals Limiting

A limiter is similar to a compressor, except that it provides a ceiling past which the peak volumes will not exceed. This allows the average volume, known as the perceived loudness, to be increased. The result is a much narrower dynamic range and a louder-sounding master. Cubase has a very capable mastering limiter called the Maximizer.

Contemporary Mastering and the Loudness War

The "loud" adjective in the mastering equation is the subject of much debate. Over the past few decades, the availability and use (or overuse) of software-based mastering limiters have succeeded in stripping most of the dynamics from popular music. The phenomenon has become so pervasive that it's been added to the English lexicon. It's known as the Loudness War. To illustrate this phenomenon, I'm going to load some CD tracks into Cubase and analyze their average or perceived loudness. You can do the same thing by importing an audio CD track into Cubase by clicking the File menu, selecting Import, and then selecting Audio CD. After the track is imported, you can click on the Audio event, and select Statistics from the Audio menu.

   (Note: Copyright, not to mention karma, prevents me from including any of the source material on the disc that comes with this book. You'll have to use music from your library for your own analyses.)

Comparing the Evolution of Loudness

In Figure 8.1, I've imported four CD tracks from different musical eras. Take a look at the differences in volume as depicted by their event waveform displays.

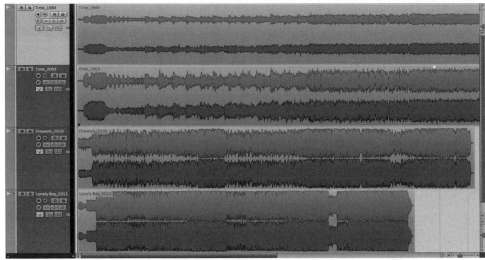

Figure 8.1: Four audio CD tracks imported into Cubase

The top two tracks are different masters of Pink Floyd's "Time" from *Dark Side of the Moon*. The top track is from the original 1984 CD release and is virtually identical to the original LP release from 1973. The next track is the same song, but comes from the 2003 thirtieth-anniversary remaster. They certainly look different, don't they? Track 3 has the 2010 release of Katy Perry's "Firework," and track 4 is the Black Keys' "Lonely Boy" from 2011. Do you see how the volume has increased over the decades? But to what degree? To find out, I'm going to select the "Time_1984" event and choose Statistics from the Audio menu. The results are in Figure 8.2.

Channel	Left	Right
Min. Sample Value:	−0.443	−0.494
	−7.07 dB	−6.13 dB
Max. Sample Value:	0.484	0.452
	−6.30 dB	−6.89 dB
Peak Amplitude:	−6.30 dB	−6.13 dB
DC Offset:	2.03 %	1.64 %
	−59.36 dB	−60.63 dB
Estimated Resolution:	16 Bit	16 Bit
Estimated Pitch:	1351.5Hz/E5	1444.2Hz/F#5
Sample Rate:	44.100 kHz	44.100 kHz
Min. RMS Power:	−54.86 dB	−54.70 dB
Max. RMS Power:	−16.73 dB	−16.76 dB
Average:	−22.91 dB	−22.28 dB

Statistics – "Time_1984"

Close

Figure 8.2: Statistical analysis of "Time" from 1984

Notice the values outlined in the box. What we're looking at is the Maximum RMS (Root Mean Squared) Power and Average volume. These are used to determine the perceived loudness of the left and right audio channels. When we average the left and right channels together, we get a perceived volume of –22.5 dB below zero. When "Time" was remastered in 2003, the perceived loudness increased. Figure 8.3 shows the statistics from the "Time_2003" event.

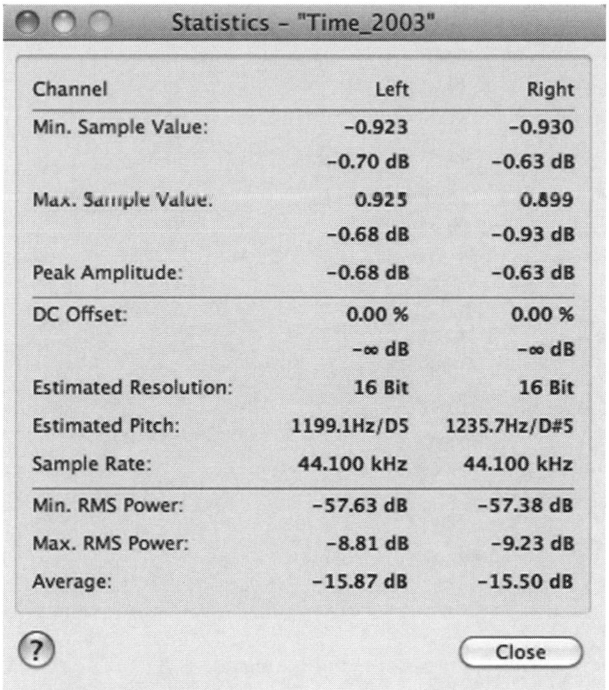

Channel	Left	Right
Statistics – "Time_2003"		
Min. Sample Value:	-0.923	-0.930
	-0.70 dB	-0.63 dB
Max. Sample Value:	0.925	0.899
	-0.68 dB	-0.93 dB
Peak Amplitude:	-0.68 dB	-0.63 dB
DC Offset:	0.00 %	0.00 %
	-∞ dB	-∞ dB
Estimated Resolution:	16 Bit	16 Bit
Estimated Pitch:	1199.1Hz/D5	1235.7Hz/D#5
Sample Rate:	44.100 kHz	44.100 kHz
Min. RMS Power:	-57.63 dB	-57.38 dB
Max. RMS Power:	-8.81 dB	-9.23 dB
Average:	-15.87 dB	-15.50 dB

Figure 8.3: Statistical analysis of "Time" from 2003

Now the average has jumped from –22.5 to –15.7 dB below zero, an increase in perceived loudness of almost 7 dB. It's the same song but with different mastering outcomes, particularly in perceived loudness. Now take a look at Figure 8.4 that shows the statistics for "Firework."

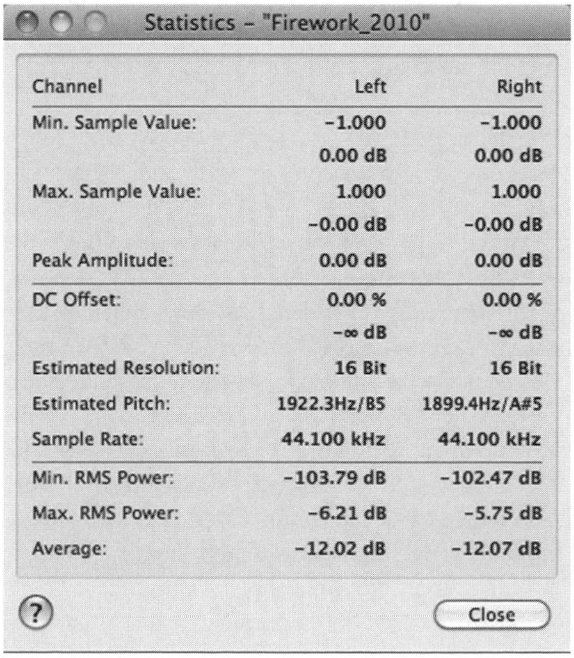

Channel	Left	Right
Statistics – "Firework_2010"		
Min. Sample Value:	-1.000	-1.000
	0.00 dB	0.00 dB
Max. Sample Value:	1.000	1.000
	-0.00 dB	-0.00 dB
Peak Amplitude:	0.00 dB	0.00 dB
DC Offset:	0.00 %	0.00 %
	-∞ dB	-∞ dB
Estimated Resolution:	16 Bit	16 Bit
Estimated Pitch:	1922.3Hz/B5	1899.4Hz/A#5
Sample Rate:	44.100 kHz	44.100 kHz
Min. RMS Power:	-103.79 dB	-102.47 dB
Max. RMS Power:	-6.21 dB	-5.75 dB
Average:	-12.02 dB	-12.07 dB

Figure 8.4: Statistical analysis of "Firework" from 2010

The average jumps up to –12.0 dB below zero, which means "Firework," like many popular songs of today, doesn't have a wide dynamic range. Finally, look at Figure 8.5, which shows the statistics for "Lonely Boy."

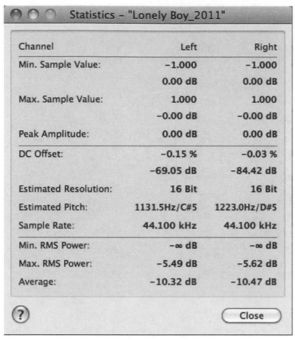

Statistics – "Lonely Boy_2011"		
Channel	**Left**	**Right**
Min. Sample Value:	–1.000	–1.000
	0.00 dB	0.00 dB
Max. Sample Value:	1.000	1.000
	–0.00 dB	–0.00 dB
Peak Amplitude:	0.00 dB	0.00 dB
DC Offset:	–0.15 %	–0.03 %
	–69.05 dB	–84.42 dB
Estimated Resolution:	16 Bit	16 Bit
Estimated Pitch:	1131.5Hz/C#5	1223.0Hz/D#5
Sample Rate:	44.100 kHz	44.100 kHz
Min. RMS Power:	–∞ dB	–∞ dB
Max. RMS Power:	–5.49 dB	–5.62 dB
Average:	–10.32 dB	–10.47 dB

Figure 8.5: Statistical analysis of "Lonely Boy" from 2011

As I write this book, "Lonely Boy" is the #1 song on the *Billboard* Rock Song chart. It's a great song by a great band. But as you can see, the average is up to –10.4 dB below zero. Suffice it to say that the perceived loudness of pop music has been increasing year by year.

Daring to Be Different

I like a lot of different genres of music. I especially enjoy going to live performances of symphony orchestras, especially if they're performing Mahler, Bach, Orff, or Holst. But no matter what is on the program, I'm sure to experience a wide dynamic range, from triple *pianissimo* to triple *forte*.

Well, it appears that contemporary pop music is all triple *forte*. That doesn't leave much room for the dynamics to be as useful as the melody, lyrics, chord progression, or beat. But humans actually do enjoy wide dynamic range. If we didn't, we wouldn't go to firework shows. Can you imagine how boring it would be to have the explosions be roughly the same volume as the background noise of cars and conversation?

With that in mind, I'm going to dare you to be different when mastering your music or that of your clients. Figure 8.3 shows an average volume of –15.7 dB below zero. That's about the average level I try to achieve when mastering music for my own personal enjoyment. However, I usually master another version that gets closer to –13 or even –12 dB below zero. This is because my song may end up played on the radio or on someone's MP3 player with a bunch of other music, and I don't want listeners to be constantly adjusting their volume control. Of course, if clients request that their music approach the average volume of –10 dB below zero or even higher, I will do as they ask. But if I really like their music, I may make some private mixes with a wider dynamic range for myself.

But the realization that every audio device in history has had a volume control throws the idea of the Loudness War into irrelevance. It may take some time, but I hope that in the future, the listening public will demand a wider dynamic range. Since car stereos, home entertainment systems, and MP3 players all have their own volume controls with which to control the volume level, maybe we should trust the listener to have the final say in how loudly the music should be played.

Note: Different audio software programs (such as Cubase and WaveLab) will analyze and report the average volumes in different ways. Therefore, when making your own analyses, always use the same program, and don't mix those results with those from a different program.

The March Toward the Master Fader

For the rest of this chapter, you could certainly apply mastering processes to your own Cubase Project. However, if you'd like to follow along with me, make sure you load the "The Right Track Matt R09.cpr" project from the disc that came with this book. (See appendix A, "Using the Included Disc.") Since we've used that project throughout this book, you may have noticed that the signal flows through the mixer from left to right. In other words, Audio and Instrument channels come first, followed by Group channels, and finally FX Channel tracks. An example of this can be seen in Figure 8.6.

Figure 8.6: Signal flow through the Mixer to the Master Fader

The concept is that every track, channel, and VST plug-in will eventually be routed to the Master Fader. And whatever you are monitoring from the Master Fader is what will eventually be delivered to the ears of the end-listener.

Examining the Master Fader

A closer look at the Master Fader in the Mixer will reveal how similar it is to an Audio, Instrument, Group, or FX channel. However, there are a few differences that are better illustrated by clicking the Master Fader Edit button to open the VST Channel Settings window, as shown in Figure 8.7.

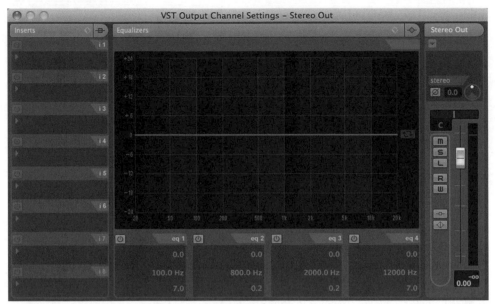

Figure 8.7: VST Channel Settings window of Master Fader

The most obvious difference between the Master Fader and any other channel is a lack of Sends and a Sends Bypass button. That's because the Master Fader is the final destination for any output channel. There is also no input setting in the Routing section for the same reason. However, many of the other controls with which we're already familiar are present. The Inserts are where we'll apply certain mastering plug-ins; the EQ is what we'll use to craft the overall tonality of the project; and Inserts 7 and 8 come after the Master Fader, into which we'll install a mastering limiter and a dithering plug-in. (More on dithering later.)

Adjusting the Master Fader Level

The Master Fader also controls the volume of the mixdown. If it's set too low, the mixdown will be quieter than it should be. However, if it's set too high, the Master Fader, and therefore the mixdown, can become clipped. Whether you're mixing to audio file, audio CD, or MP3, clipping will compromise, if not ruin, your mixdown. Cubase has several facilities with which to monitor and adjust the Master Fader for the loudest, clipping-free mixdown level.

Peak Meter Value

Figure 8.8:
Master Fader and
Transport Panel
Master Fader
controls

There are two numeric values that appear at the bottom of the Master Fader. The value at the bottom with a larger font is the Channel Level that shows the position of the Master Fader. But above the Channel Level is the Peak Meter Value in a slightly smaller font. Both of these values are shown in Figure 8.8.

The Peak Meter Value is constantly monitoring the peak output level of your Cubase Project. The value depicts the loudest peak that was encountered during playback. Figure 8.8 shows the peak value of the R09 version of our project. That value is 0.9 dB above zero. Zero, as you probably already know, is the maximum output level. Therefore, any value above zero indicates clipping. Similarly, a negative value might indicate too low a Master Fader setting. For example, a value of –1.0 would indicate an appropriate Master Fader setting, but –10.0 would result in a very quiet mixdown. The best way to use the Peak Meter Value is to click it to reset it to –∞ (infinity, or absolute silence). Then start playback from the beginning of the project and continue through to the end of the project. The Peak Meter Value displays the loudest volume encountered during project playback.

Whether the value is positive or negative will determine the appropriate action. (More on that in a moment.)

Clip Indicators

Clipping results in audible distortion and occurs when the maximum output level is pushed beyond the maximum limit of 0 dB. Recording in 32-bit floating point gives your Cubase Project an astronomically wide internal dynamic range, and also makes it impossible to clip the signal flow within Cubase. That is, until the signal reaches the Master Fader; when it clips, your mixdown will also be clipped.

Cubase has a clipping indicator that is shown in two different locations: the bottom of the Master Fader and the right side of the Transport Panel. (See Figure 8.8.) When the Peak Meter Value has exceeded 0 dB, the clip indicators glow red. The indicator or the Master Fader also has a "CLIP" readout. You can reset the clip indicators by clicking on them, which will also reset the Peak Meter Value to −∞ dB. If you've followed the procedure of determining the maximum Peak Meter Value and the clip indicator has turned red, it means you need to make a Master Fader adjustment.

Adjusting the Master Fader for Optimal Audio Mixdown Level

There are two different ways to adjust the output level of the Master Fader. The first one is easy: just move the Fader up or down or type the desired value into the Channel Level. (See Figure 8.8.) But I prefer using the Input Gain controls at the top of the Master Fader in the Routing View. You can do so by holding the Shift key on your computer keyboard while adjusting the Input Gain knob, or you can double-click the Input Gain value and type in the desired value. I prefer this method because of the mastering process we're about to undertake. By adjusting the Input Gain, you're also optimizing the signal level of the Insert slots, and that's where most of the mastering plug-ins will be installed. Therefore, prior to mastering, I'll set the Master Fader to its default 0.00 dB below zero position, then play the project from start to finish. When the Peak Meter value has been determined, I enter the opposite of that value into the Input Gain value. In other words, if the Peak Meter Value is 0.9 (a positive value), I'll enter −1.0 or −1.1 (negative values) into the Input Gain value. That way, I'll have a few tenths of a dB (undetectable by the human ear) for a safety margin.

The Importance of Setting the Master Fader Prior to Mastering

You may have asked yourself why we set the Master Fader before we started applying mastering plug-ins. The first reason is to set an optimal signal flow through the Insert slots and then to the Master Fader. But the main reason is that if someone else is going to be doing your mastering (or if you plan to do the mastering in a different program, such as WaveLab), you'll want a premastered mixdown in WAV or AIFF format. That mixdown should be void of any Inserts or EQs on the Master Fader and should also be set to the optimal output level. We'll explore this more when we export our mixdowns later in this chapter.

Applying the Mastering Plug-ins

Now that we've optimized our Master Fader output level, it's time to experiment with some mastering plug-ins and associated settings. It's critical during the mastering process to be constantly listening to the playback. Unlike some other programs, Cubase allows you to assign plug-ins during playback, but you will notice a slight audio dropout. That shouldn't concern you, as it is normal, and it sure beats having to repeatedly hit Stop and Play. For the following example, we're going to use my "punchy, shiny, and LOUD" method for mastering. That will mean using the Master Fader section for the application of the MultibandCompressor, EQ, and Maximizer.

Keeping Your Ears Honest

Before proceeding, you should know a few important rules that will help you achieve great mastering results no matter what the end-listener is using for playback. First and foremost, do not allow your monitor speaker volume to exceed an average output level of 85 dB. We all like to hear the music nice and loud. However, levels above 85 dB, even for a short amount of time, will color the way our ears hear the music. But levels below 85 dB will not allow us to hear enough audio detail. Do yourself a favor and get an SPL (Sound Pressure Level) meter to determine your monitor speaker volume. Or if you have an iPod touch, iPhone, or iPad, go to the App Store and check out the Audio Tool from Performance Audio. It's only a few bucks, looks really cool, and among its other tools, it has a great SPL meter called Decibel Meter Pro.

And speaking of speakers, you'll also need a good pair of studio monitors. The prices for these specialized speakers have come down considerably, making them affordable as well as indispensible. Don't try to use headphones, the speakers that came with your computer, or any consumer-grade speakers such as those of a home stereo system. They don't sound very accurate and will lie to your ears. Also make sure the speakers are placed at ear level (not above or below your eye line) and arranged in an equilateral triangle, as shown in Figure 8.9.

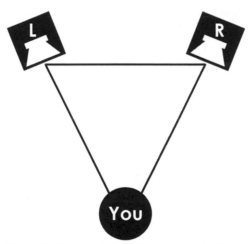

Figure 8.9: Overhead view of proper speaker/head arrangement

Finally, grab some commercially released music from bands and/or genres that match the music you're mastering. In other words, if you're mastering a country project, grab some Brad Paisley or Shania Twain CDs. Basically, grab the best-sounding CDs from a like genre, and keep them handy for comparison. That way you can compare the mastering of a popular band or artist to that of your own.

A Word About Headphones

When you try to mix or master using headphones, you'll lose one of the most important aspects of stereo sound: proper phase alignment. Because headphones place the speakers so close to your eardrum, they don't allow you to discern how the sound travels through the air to both ears, making it impossible to hear phase problems. Therefore, you should not use headphones as your only speaker during the mixing or mastering processes.

However, I will make one exception: i-device earbuds. I'm talking about the white earbuds that come with every Apple iPod and iPhone. If you're like me, you listened to them and upgraded to a better pair, or you were already aware of how unspectacular they sound and never unwrapped them. If you still have them, they might serve a useful purpose here. At the end of a mastering session and before I perform the mixdown, I'll listen to how it sounds on the earbuds. That's because many end-listeners out there still use their original earbuds. This allows me to hear how the mastered mixdown will sound to the joggers, dog-walkers, and pedestrians I see with their ubiquitous white cables dangling from their ears. The theory is: if you can make a master sound nicely balanced on studio monitors as well as earbuds, it will sound good on any audio system.

Using the MultibandCompressor

The "punchy" adjective is achieved by using the MultibandCompressor plug-in. But as you will see, you'll gain more than punch from this powerful plug-in. From the Master Fader Inserts in the Extended Mixer View or the Inserts of the VST Channel Settings window, click on Insert slot 1 (i1), select the Dynamics category, then chose MulitbandCompressor. The MultibandCompressor control panel will appear, as shown in Figure 8.10.

Figure 8.10: The MultibandCompressor control panel, Rock Master 2 preset (modified)

By default, there is no preset visible in the Preset field. However, you should be aware that the MultibandCompressor is processing the signal and the sound. Therefore, it's normal to hear the volume level jump up when you first load the plug-in. If you ever need to return to this default setting, load the preset named "Reset."

The Operation of the MultibandCompressor

An ordinary compressor operates on the full range of audio frequencies, whereas the MultibandCompressor operates as four separate frequency-based compressors. This allows you to compress each frequency band differently, which prevents a preponderance of certain frequencies from adversely affecting the volumes of others. To get a better idea of how the frequency bands are divided, click on the Solo band button (see Figure 8.10) on any of the four bands. What you'll hear are the frequencies being compressed by the associated band. The low frequencies will be mostly the rumble of bass drum and bass guitar. The low-mids will contain the fundamental frequencies of the vocals, keyboards, snare drum, and acoustic guitar. The high-mids will contain the brightness of the instruments in the low-mid band, and the tambourine becomes audible. Finally, the highs contain guitar-pick noise, the tambourine jangles, hi-hat cymbals, and the sibilance of the vocals.

Auditioning MultibandCompressor Presets

Let's listen to some of the MultibandCompressor presets. Click the Presets field (see Figure 8.10), and choose Rock Master. To my ears, the low band has a nice response, but the low and high-mid bands become too deficient, and the high band becomes too thin and bright. Now try the Rock Master 2 preset. Suddenly the lows are nice and punchy, plus the acoustic guitar and the vocals (low-mid band) become more pronounced. The highs are also nicely tamed. I like this preset, so let's go with that. However, you'll notice that the Output Level on the control panel is set to 2.2 dB. That has increased the overall volume level, and the clip indicators are lit because of it. Therefore, enter a value of 0.0. (See Figure 8.10.) The volume will drop a bit, but don't worry, because we'll be adjusting the "LOUD" a little later.

Now click the Bypass button at the top of the control panel to audition the before and after of the MultibandCompressor. The before sounds kind of vague and undefined, whereas the after has more definition, and the mix is punching through your speakers to your ears. As you can see, the MultibandCompressor is more than punchy low frequencies. It can be used to craft a smoother volume response across all the frequency bands. That makes our EQ task quite a bit easier.

Using the Master Fader EQ

After the signal flows out of the MultibandCompressor (or the last plug-in installed in Inserts 1 through 6), it goes into the Master Fader EQ. This is the same 4-band, fully parametric EQ you've used on Audio, Instrument, Group, and FX channels, so you're already familiar with how it works. In the context of mastering, EQ is where you can craft the tonality, not of a single channel, but of the entire mix. Since the EQ is part of the Master Fader channel, we don't need to assign a plug-in.

Adjusting the EQ Parameters

This is where we can add the "shiny" quality to the master. After some careful listening and comparison to other commercial masters, I came up with the EQ curve shown in Figure 8.11.

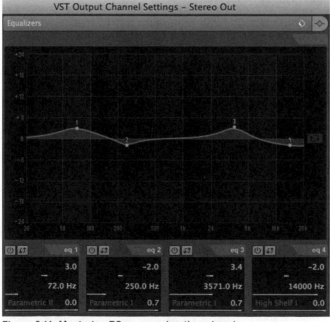

Figure 8.11: Mastering EQ curve using three bands

The first thing I wanted to hear was a few more high-mids, so I increased EQ 3 to 3.5 dB at 3,570 Hz. Then I noticed a little throatiness in the low-mids, so I decreased EQ 2 –2.0 dB at 250 Hz. But I wanted a little more low end, so I switched EQ 1 to the Parametric II filter and added 3.0 dB at 72 Hz. Then I compared that to some like genres and determined that the whole mix sounded a little too shiny. So I set the highs of EQ 4 to a High Shelf I filter type and decreased the frequencies above 14,000 Hz by 2.0 dB. That also helped add a little analog-like warmth. But your results may vary; feel free to try your own settings.

Using the Maximizer

This is how we add the "LOUD" quality to our master. While the Maximizer mastering limiter that comes with Cubase is technically not a "brick wall" limiter, it still does a nice job of increasing the average volumes. This is also where we utilize Insert 7, because it comes after the Master Fader. (We're saving Insert 8 for later.) Click on Insert slot 7 (i7), and choose Maximizer from the Dynamics category. Compared to the other mastering treatments, the Maximizer has a very simple control panel, as shown in Figure 8.12.

Up until we installed the Maximizer, the Master Fader was the final destination of our mixdown. But now the output-level control of the Maximizer serves that purpose. Notice in Figure 8.12 that I've set the output to –0.2 dB below zero. That sets a safety that limits the total output of the mixdown to two-tenths of a decibel below zero, and ensures that CD players and other audio devices don't distort when decoding audio signals above –0.1 or 0.0 dB. (I've found a few commercial CDs that will distort certain CD players yet sound fine when played in others. One example is the Rush album *Vapor Trails*.) The soft clip button is on by default, which provides a more gentle type of limiting. However, if you're mastering loud, edgy music, such as industrial metal or dub step, you might want to disable soft clip. All that leaves is adjusting the Optimize control, which determines the perceived loudness of the mixdown. Or another way to look at it is by asking, "To what degree shall I fight in the Loudness War?" The default is 25.0, but if the master was for me, I'd set it to 0.0 (which will still lightly limit the output and leave the maximum at –0.2 dB). But if I needed the mix to compete with contemporary music, I'd go for as high as possible without the sound becoming too crushed. In this example, I found that 29.0 was an appropriate setting.

Figure 8.12: The Maximizer control panel

Take a Moment to Listen and Save

Now that our mix is a punchy, shiny, and LOUD master, let's listen to the before and after of the mastering processes. The easiest way to do this is to use the Insert and EQ Bypass buttons. (See Figure 8.7.) When they are bypassed, we're hearing the original mix. When enabled, we're hearing the mastered version. The difference can be a little startling. The mixed version, while sounding fine, definitely lacks some of the refinement and impact of the mastered version. Now is a good time to save this version of the project, which I've already done as version R10. But since R10 is already in your Project Folder, I'm going to have you save it as R11.

Exporting the Audio Mixdown, Times Three

Now that we've mixed and mastered our project, it's time to export it as a mixdown that we can share with the world. But to do it right, we'll need to save three different versions. This is because you should always execute your mixdown for three contingencies.

First, you'll want a high-bit-rate version that matches the Bit Resolution (Project menu, Project Setup window) of your recorded tracks. In other words, if you recorded your Audio tracks in 32-bit float, you'll want a 32-bit-float mixdown. This version should also be void of all mastering plug-ins and EQ. This will provide you with a "future proof" mixdown that you can give to another mastering engineer, or the ability to remaster the original mix at any later date. Without this file, you'd have to remix and remaster the same project in Cubase, and there's no guarantee that future versions of Cubase, the plug-ins, the operating system, or the computer will be able to load this Cubase Project file.

Second, you'll want an audio CD–compatible file that you can burn onto an audio CD. This version should include the mastering processes but needs to be 16-bit resolution. If the project was originally recorded in 24- or 32-bit, you'll need to dither the mixdown to 16-bit for audio CD. It's a very easy process that we'll discuss in a moment. (Note: If you recorded your tracks at a higher sample rate than 44.1 kHz, you'll need to convert it to 44.1 before it can be burned to an audio CD.)

Lastly, you'll want an MP3 version for email, Internet, and ecommerce purposes. These are much smaller than the WAV or AIFF versions but don't sound quite the same because of data compression. (Not to be confused with audio compression.) That data compression does alter the sound characteristics, but MP3 files can be easily shared via email, uploaded to websites, or submitted for sale to cdbaby.com, iTunes, and so forth. With that in mind, let's make some mixdowns.

Setting the Left and Right Locators

The Locators are used for a myriad of different purposes during the recording and mixing processes. But for mixdown, they're used to determine along the Time Ruler the project starts and ends. Let me show you an easy way to set the Locators for mixdown. From the Project window, I'm going to type Ctrl/Command + A, which will select all of the events in the Event Display. Then I'm going to type "P" (Locators to Selection) on my computer keyboard, which will place the Left Locator at the earliest event boundary and the Right Locator at the latest event boundary, as shown in Figure 8.13.

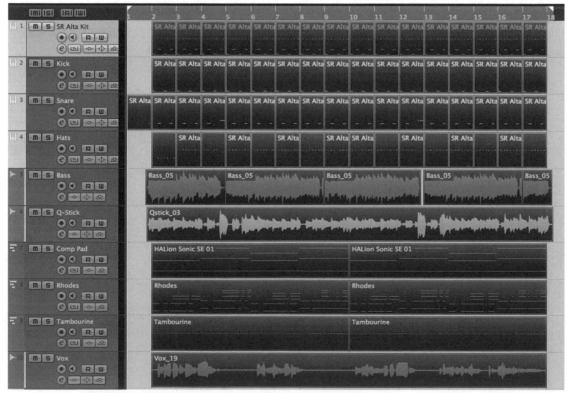

Figure 8.13: Results of the Locators to Selection command

We could perform the audio export now, but we'd have a couple of problems. The first of which is that there would be quite a bit of silence before the song started. The left event boundary does not have any notes until the fourth beat of measure 1. It would be better to move the Left Locator (with Snap off) slightly to the left of that first note. Similarly, since we're using a delay and reverb in this project, it's conceivable that the audio produced by those time-based effects will continue past the Right Locator. To that end, move the Right Locator a few more beats to the right. In the case of this project, the downbeat of measure 19 would do nicely.

Mixdown #1: High Bit Rate with No Mastering

Before proceeding, let's determine the bit resolution of the project. Click the Project menu, and choose Project Setup. Look for the Bit Resolution setting. In this case, it's 32-Bit Float. Now we know that our high-bit-rate version should also be in 32-Bit Float format. Then click both the Insert and EQ Bypass buttons on the Master Fader. (See Figure 8.7.) Then click the File menu, select Export, and choose Audio Mixdown. The Export Audio Mixdown dialog box will appear, as shown in Figure 8.14.

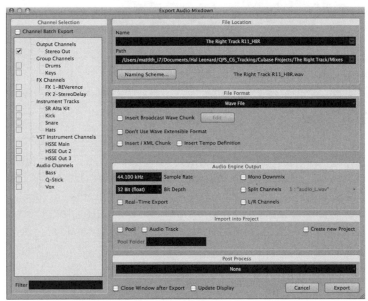

Figure 8.14: The Export Audio Mixdown dialog box

Make sure that the Stereo Out is enabled under Channel Selection. Then set the Sample Rate to 44.100 kHz (or the sample rate of the project as shown in the Project Setup window) and the Bit Depth to 32-Bit (Float) (or the bit resolution in the Project Setup window). Then type in the desired file name. I include the revision number of the project, then an underscore, then HBR to indicate this as the high-bit-rate mixdown. Then click the Path button, and select Choose. A standard file navigation box will appear. I recommend choosing the Project Folder you created when you started the project, then creating a new folder called "Mixes." I set the File Format to Wave File (WAV or Microsoft Wave Format) and then verify that all of the checkboxes (other than Stereo Out) are disabled. Then hit the Export button. The mixdown will usually proceed in faster than real-time speed, but that depends largely on the complexity of the project and the speed of your computer. (If you want to hear the project in real-time during the export, enable the Real-Time Export checkbox.) When the export is complete, the window will stay open, allowing us to export our next mixdown.

Mixdown #2: Audio CD–Compatible with Mastering

Return to the mixer, and enable the Inserts and EQ buttons. (See Figure 8.7.) But if the project bit resolution was higher than 16-bit (and in the case of this example project, it was), we'd need to dither down to 16-bit. As weird as that might sound, it's much easier than you think.

Using the Apogee UV22HR Dithering Plug-in

The more digital bits you use, the wider your dynamic range. That's why at 32-bit, Cubase has a huge dynamic range of 1,536 dB. But audio CDs are 16-bit with a dynamic range of 96 dB. If we don't dither the mixdown, Cubase will unceremoniously lop off half the bits. But with the Apogee UV22HR (the dithering plug-in that comes with Cubase), the dithering process will analyze which of the 16-bits most accurately represent the original audio stream and uses them to export the audio. All you need to do is click on Master Fader Insert Slot 8 (i8, see Figure 8.7), select the Mastering category, and select UV22HR. The control panel will appear, as shown in Figure 8.15.

Figure 8.15: The UV22HR dithering plug-in with audio CD–compatible settings

There are only two buttons to click: 16 and hi. Believe it or not, that's it. However, if you're sending your mixdowns to another mastering engineer, it would be wise to ask him or her what bit resolution he or she wants the file in. Not all audio programs are capable of recognizing 32-bit files. Therefore, you might need to use the UV22HR output bits set to 24 or even 16 depending on his or her answer, but the Inserts and EQ would also need to be disabled to allow for proper second-party mastering.

Proceeding with the Mixdown

All you need to do now is change the File name and Bit Depth (and possibly the sample rate to 44.1 kHz) in the Export Audio Mixdown window. (See Figure 8.14.) I used the same naming convention as before, except this time I changed "HBR" to "16" to indicate that this is a 16-bit version. "(The Right Track R10_16.") Then set the Bit Depth to 16 Bit, and click the Export button.

Mixdown #3: MP3 Version

For this version, you'll need to leave the UV22HR on. But you'll need to change the Name to include only the name of the song, and you'll need to change the File Format from Wave File (see Figure 8.14) to MPEG 1 Layer 3 File, as shown in Figure 8.16.

Figure 8.16: MPEG 1 Layer 3 File format

The settings in the File Format section will change to include MP3 specific settings, the most important of which is the Bit Rate slider. This is used to balance the file size to the audio quality. Increasing the slider will provide a higher-quality sound but with increased file size. Lowering the slider will make the file smaller and easier to download over slow Internet connections but will also degrade the sound quality. With the continual increase in Internet speeds, I would recommend a bit rate of no lower than 256 kBit. That will create a good-sounding file with a manageable file size.

You can disable the High Quality mode, although I can't think of a good reason to do so. While not compulsory, I would recommend enabling the Insert ID3 tag option and then clicking the Edit ID3 Tab button. The ID3 Tag window will appear, as shown in Figure 8.17.

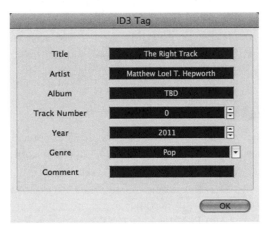

Figure 8.17: The ID3 Tag window

If you've used a program such as iTunes or Windows Media Player, you'll certainly recognize these fields. The ID3 tags are what appear in the information section of a media player program. So it's a good idea to fill in the appropriate fields. For example, the File Name does not necessarily equal the Title field. This allows you to reference the song by title name or file name. The other fields should be filled in accordingly, and you can see the examples I've used for this project in Figure 8.17. When finished, click OK, and click the Export button on the Export Audio Mixdown window.

Examining the Results

Now that your project has been mixed to the three file formats, you can close Cubase and view the contents of your Project Folder, as shown in Figure 8.18.

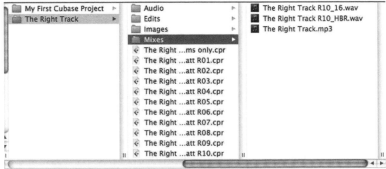

Figure 8.18: The Project Folder with Mixes folder and mixdown files

The look of the Project Folder will be different on Mac or PC, but the file hierarchy is identical to that of Figure 8.18. It's a good idea to listen to each file before certifying it finished. That will prevent you from delivering versions with errors or glitches. It's rare, but you've already listened to the song about a million times, so three more won't hurt you. It's also a good idea to load the MP3 version into iTunes or any other program that reads ID3 tags to verify the information, spelling, and so forth.

Finally, perform a statistical analysis on the 16-bit mastered version to compare the loudness to that of other commercially released music. For the R10 version of the project we've been using for this chapter, we get an average volume of –12.3 dB, which is exactly what I was going for.

Optional Mixdown #4: High Bit Rate with Mastering

It's not a bad idea to create a high-bit-rate version that includes all the mastering plug-ins. However, I've found that if I get the urge to do any remastering, I'll load the original HBR file into a new Cubase Project (or a mastering program such as WaveLab) and start the mastering from scratch. There's a possibility that listening to the song after few months or years, I'll want to start the mastering from scratch and try some different treatments or even new plug-ins. That's why I choose not to perform this type of mixdown.

Backing Up Your Work

We're done, right? *Wrong*! It is critical that you take a moment to back up your project. And since I've taught you the proper Cubase media-management model, it's incredibly easy to do. Simply drag the Project Folder to your backup hard drive. You could also use optical media such as a DVD for backup purposes, but they're much more fragile than hard drives, which are getting cheaper by the minute. In fact, because I have had hard drives crash before I'm finished with a project, I regularly back up the Project Folder to a backup hard disk during the recording, editing, mixing, and mastering processes. Why take a chance?

The Concept of Onsite and Offsite Backup

Once you've backed up your Cubase Project(s), that's good but not good enough. Unfortunately, disasters happen, and I could recite from a long list of tragedies that have eaten irreplaceable data, including hard disk failures, robberies, fires, floods, and even vengeful spouses. (Now is a good time to knock on wood.) Since I've learned my lesson (more than once), I keep one hard disk (usually an external USB, FireWire, or eSATA version) at my studio and another hard disk with the same data at home. That way, if disaster strikes at one location, I still have another backup. The moral of the story is: back it up or pack it up. Consider this my urgent plea for your promise to back up your Cubase Projects. I would hate to learn that you've lost your hard work for any reason. This is your final warning. (Cue ominous music, then back that up too.)

Moving Forward

Are you ready for some good news? Now that we're at the end of this book, you'll never have to listen to "The Right Track Matt" ever again. (Don't let me see your look of relief.) However, it does mean that you're on your own, but hopefully, I've enriched you with more knowledge that will make the process of creating music easier. It has been my distinct honor to show you how to use Cubase. It is a fantastic program, and I hope you use it to create wonderful music for the world to hear. Cubase is also a very deep program, and content limits prevented me from going over all of its many facets. In fact, each one of these chapters could have been a book unto itself had I the room to do so. Alas, however, our time together has come to an end. But please keep trying other Cubase features on your own. It's software, you can't break it, so go for broke.

Appendix A: Using the Included Disc

On the enclosed disc, you will find the Cubase Projects I used throughout the book. The project we'll be using the most is "The Right Track Matt RXX.cpr." I have no doubt you will grow intensely bored of that song. (I sure have.) But the sooner you learn the techniques for editing and mixing that and the other projects on the disc, the sooner you can move on to your own material. There are detailed references to all these projects throughout the book, but let me explain a little bit more about them here.

Copying the Files to Your Computer

When you put the disc into your computer's optical drive and view its directory, you will see a folder called Cubase Projects HL. This is to differentiate it from the default Cubase Projects Folder that is created on your computer hard disk during the installation of Cubase. I would recommend copying the folder to your computer. The total size of the folder content is less than 600 MB, so it won't take much space. While you could load and play the Cubase Projects HL folder from the disc, the slow speed of an optical drive will be a problem. Take a moment to copy the folder to a location on your computer where you can easily find it.

Cubase Projects

Inside the Cubase Projects HL folder, you will find six Project Folders. Loading the projects contained within each Project Folder will allow you to see the features in Cubase that I was using while I was writing the book. Some Project Folders will contain multiple Project files (.cpr) with different revision numbers at the end of their file names (R01, R02, etc.). These are to differentiate the progress of each project. I use this as my standard methodology while working on any Cubase Project so that I can always refer to an earlier version. All of the MIDI or Instrument tracks are using HALion Sonic SE, which is one of the Cubase built-in virtual synthesizers.

A Word About the Audio Tracks

I had a dilemma when deciding how to record the Audio tracks for this book. Part of me wanted to hire studio musicians to come to my studio and lay down some truly wonderful tracks. But the editors reminded me that we needed to stay within budget and keep the book affordable. I also realized the benefit of providing you with tracks that are not—how shall I say it—Grammy winners. Therefore, I recorded all the tracks myself at my home studio using only one entry-level microphone: an AKG C3000S. This was to provide you with the same types of recordings you're creating in your home-studio environment.

The guitar and bass tracks were recorded direct (instrument plugged directly into the audio interface) to a Steinberg MR816CSX audio interface without any additional processing between the source and the audio interface. The bass was a Status S2 Classic with EMG 40TW pickups, and the guitar was a Rainsong WS1000 acoustic guitar with a Fishman pickup.

I have no doubt that you will be able to create recordings and mixes that will equal or surpass the quality of those found in these projects. But I also don't want you to fall into the trap of thinking, "I won't record Audio tracks until I get a (insert expensive audio product here)." It's better to record everything and record often, no matter what microphones, processors, or instruments you have at your disposal.

APPENDIX B: A PRIMER ON AUTOMATION

When we started to tally up the page totals of this book, it became apparent that I had gone overboard. I had fully intended to provide a chapter dedicated to automation, but we just ran out of space. While I didn't use any in the projects you'll be using (see appendix A, "Using the Included Disc"), I do feel it necessary to cover the basics of automation with this primer.

The Concept of Automation

When I say *automation*, what I'm referring to is programming the movement of the buttons, sliders, switches, and knobs in Cubase. Automation allows you to create virtual hands that can manipulate Cubase controls over the timeline of a project. The automation

in Cubase is much more powerful and effective than the traditional method, which usually involved all band members hovering over the mixer and tweaking the controls during the mixdown. Modern DAW automation also reduces the animosity between band members when one forgot to move his or her assigned slider at the right time. I've even seen a few mix sessions devolve into all-out fist fights. Let's reduce the possibility of that by exploring the benefits of automation.

The Read and Write Enable Buttons

Once you've seen the Read and Write enable buttons, you'll start seeing them everywhere in Cubase. Sometimes they're on the Cubase Mixer, while other times they're on the control panel of a VST plug-in, as shown in Figure B.1.

When Write is enabled, it means that any knob, button, slider, or parameter that gets moved during playback (you needn't be in Record mode or recording for automation programming) will be written into the corresponding Automation track. (More on Automation tracks in a moment.) The controls will then reenact the movement during playback, but only when Read is enabled.

Figure B.1: The ubiquitous Read and Write automation enable buttons

The Automation Tracks

All tracks (MIDI, Instrument, Audio, Group, and FX Channel) and the Master Fader have their own Automation tracks. By default, they're hidden to prevent an inordinate number of additional tracks in the Track Column. To reveal the Automation Lanes, hover your mouse over the lower left corner of a track. The normally invisible Show/Hide Automation button will appear, as shown in Figure B.2.

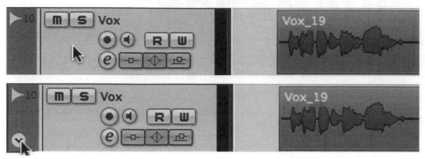

Figure B.2: Revealing the Show/Hide Automation button

When you click on the Show/Hide Automation button, the Automation track (or tracks) will appear directly beneath the Source track, as shown in Figure B.3.

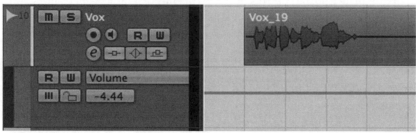

Figure B.3: The Automation track displaying volume data (default)

By default, the volume data will be shown first and appear as a horizontal line. If no automation data has been programmed, the vertical position of the data line will not vary. Note also that every Automation track has its own Read and Write buttons. They allow you to disable one specific track without affecting others. Automation tracks can also be resized for more precise editing. You can open additional Automation tracks by clicking on the Show/Hide Automation button of any visible Automation track. Another great method is Right/Ctrl-clicking any track and choosing Show All Used Automation from the submenu.

Volume *
Standard Panner – Pan Left–Right *
Input Gain
Linked Panner
Standard Panner – Pan Left–Right2
Standard Panner – Bypass
Ins.:1:Compressor – Threshold
Ins.:1:Compressor – Ratio
Ins.:1:Compressor – Attack
Ins.:1:Compressor – Release
Ins.:1:Compressor – Auto Release
Ins.:1:Compressor – Hold
Ins.:1:Compressor – MakeUp
Ins.:1:Compressor – AutoMakeUp
Ins.:1:Compressor – SoftKnee
More...

Remove Parameter
Remove Mute Automation
Remove all Automation of Track
Remove Effect Automation
Remove EQ Automation
Remove Unused Parameters
Freeze Trim

Figure B.4: The automation data selector list

Using the Data Selector

Clicking on the data selector (see Figure B.3) will allow you to choose what automation data you'd like to edit or program. Data types that have been automated will appear with an asterisk, as shown in Figure B.4.

You'll notice that volume and pan have asterisks, while the other data types don't. The most commonly automated data appear in the list, but you can also select More (see Figure B.4) to select any automatable data type.

Creating and Editing Automation Data

There are two ways to create automation data: manipulating the controls during playback (with Write Automation button enabled) or drawing the data into an Automation Lane. The latter method is preferred, as it allows you to visualize and edit the data in context with the track upon which the automation data does or will exist. To that end, let's create some automation data.

Creating Simple Automation Data

With the volume data selected and the Automation track set to Read enable, you can use your mouse in Object Selection mode to click on the horizontal automation data line. For example, in Figure B.5, I've clicked once on measure 3 and again on measure 4.

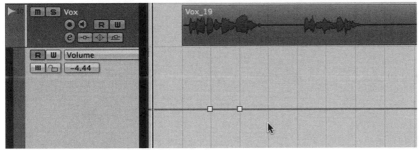

Figure B.5: Creating two automation points

Two automation points will appear as small squares on the data line. Those automation points are only visible when the mouse is hovering within the Automation track. Now you can click and drag the vertical and horizontal position of either point to automate the Volume Fader. Bear in mind that the horizontal placement of the point will be governed by the Snap setting. You can disable Snap by typing "J" on your computer keyboard.

Creating Complex Automation with the Draw and Line Tools

The Draw tool can be selected by clicking on it in the Toolbox (see Figure B.6) or by typing "8" on the upper row of number keys on your computer keyboard.

Figure B.6: The Draw and Line tools in the Toolbox, top of Project window Toolbar

With the Draw tool selected, you can click and drag across the Automation Line to create complex automation data. Similarly, you can click and hold on the Line tool to choose from five curves: Line, Parabola, Sine, Triangle, and Square. Clicking and dragging in the Automation Lane will create automation data based on the shape of the selected Line tool curve. After the data has been created, you can switch back to your Object Select tool by typing "1" on the upper row of number keys on your computer keyboard and adjusting the placement of the automation points.

Experimenting with Automation

In this primer, I've provided you with only a smattering of automation possibilities. I would urge you to experiment with different automation data on different tracks. Automation data is not permanent and can always be edited or erased. You can do this by Right/Ctrl-clicking the Automation track and choosing Select All Events from the submenu, then hitting the backspace to erase all the data on the track. You can also turn off the Read enable for the track to ignore the automation, or you can click the Mute Automation button (see Figure B.5) to temporarily or permanently disable the Automation track.

APPENDIX C: MANAGING AUDIO INTERFACE BUFFER SETTINGS

Managing the buffer size of your audio interface is critical. If you don't, both the recording and mixing processes can be severely hampered. Now that you've reached the mixing stage of your project, you'll want to increase the buffer size. This is because you'll be creating more processor-intensive virtual components during the mix, such as reverbs, delays, compressors, and other effects. The more of those you add, the larger the buffer will need to be. If the buffer is set too low, you can end up with pops, clicks, and other distortion. In this appendix, I'll show you how to adjust the buffer settings.

The Simple Rule for Determining Buffer Size

Determining the proper buffer size is simple if you follow this rule: Recording = smaller buffer sizes; mixing and mastering = larger buffer sizes. To adjust the buffer size, click the Devices menu, and select Device Setup. The Device Setup window will appear, as shown in Figure C.1.

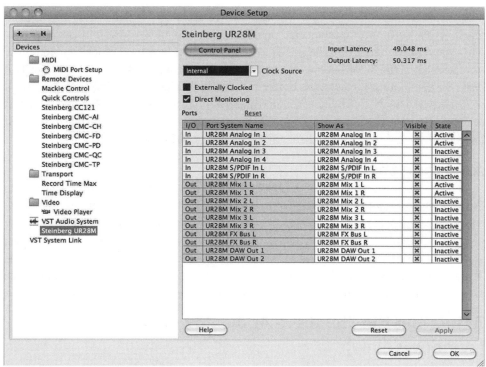

Figure C.1: The Device Setup window

You'll first need to click on the VST Audio System on the left side of the Device Setup window. Next, click on whatever appears below the VST Audio System heading. This is the make and model of your audio interface, so what is shown in Figure C.1 will be different from what you see on your window (unless you too are using a Steinberg UR28M). Then click on the Control Panel button.

Control Panel Settings (Including Latency)

Clicking on the Control Panel button will reveal another window. However, the appearance of the window and the settings themselves will be specific to your audio interface and will be different on Mac and PC, as shown in Figure C.2.

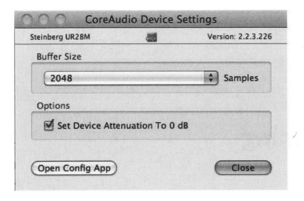
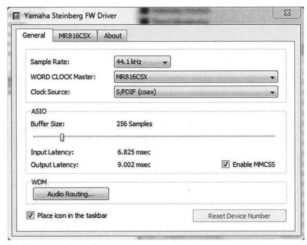

Figure C.2: Control panels: Mac (left) and Windows (right)

Since different manufacturers will design their control panels differently, I cannot speak about all the settings you might find on yours, save one: buffer size. The buffer size is what controls your audio interface latency. *Latency* is how long it takes for your computer to receive an audio signal at the interface In port, and then send it to the interface Out port. For virtual instruments, the buffer size determines how long it will take for MIDI information to be received, converted into audio by the virtual synthesizer, and then sent to the audio Out port. But during mixing, your computer will be generating the largest number of virtual devices and demanding the largest buffer size.

Adjusting the Buffer

During the mixing and mastering processes, I would recommend setting the buffer size to its maximum possible value. Don't be afraid of using 1,024 or even 2,048 samples. To do this, some control panels will have a drop-down box, while others have sliders and even knobs. Use whatever appears on your control panel to increase the buffer size. Then, when you start recording your next project, repeat the process, but try to set it as low as possible. A modern computer should be able to handle 64 or 128 samples. But if you experience pops and clicks, try 256 or 384 samples, or whatever it takes to eliminate the anomalies.

Activating the Steinberg Audio Power Scheme (Windows Only)

No matter where you are in your Cubase Project, it's a good idea, if you're using Windows, to activate the Steinberg Audio Power Scheme. This will prevent the CPUs and processor cores in your computer from being throttled. CPU throttling dynamically adjusts the speed of the CPU and the related cores based on load demand, but can cause problems for DAW programs such as Cubase. This power scheme will be active when Cubase is running, and return the computer to the Windows setting when you quit Cubase. All you need to do is enable the Activate Steinberg Audio Power Scheme checkbox on the Device Setup window, as shown in Figure C.3.

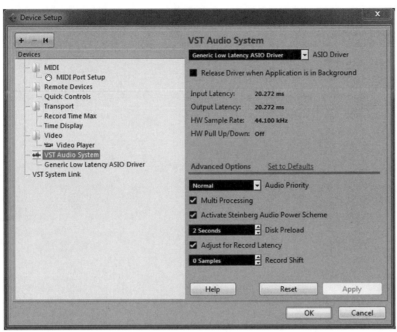

Figure C.3: The Device Setup window and Steinberg Audio Power Scheme checkbox

INDEX

quick PRO guides *series*

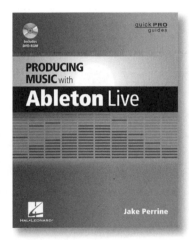

Producing Music with Ableton Live
by Jake Perrine
Softcover w/DVD-ROM •
978-1-4584-0036-9 • $16.99

Sound Design, Mixing, and Mastering with Ableton Live
by Jake Perrine
Softcover w/DVD-ROM •
978-1-4584-0037-6 • $16.99

The Power in Reason
by Andrew Eisele
Softcover w/DVD-ROM •
978-1-4584-0228-8 • $16.99

Sound Design and Mixing in Reason
by Andrew Eisele
Softcover w/DVD-ROM •
978-1-4584-0229-5 • $16.99

Mixing and Mastering with Pro Tools
by Glenn Lorbecki
Softcover w/DVD-ROM •
978-1-4584-0033-8 •$16.99

Tracking Instruments and Vocals with Pro Tools
by Glenn Lorbecki
Softcover w/DVD-ROM •
978-1-4584-0034-5 •$16.99

The Power in Logic Pro: Songwriting, Composing, Remixing, and Making Beats
by Dot Bustelo
Softcover w/DVD-ROM •
78-1-4584-1419-9 • $16.99

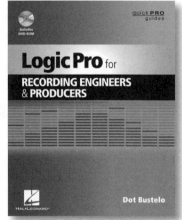

Logic Pro for Recording Engineers and Producers
by Dot Bustelo
Softcover w/DVD-ROM •
978-1-4584-1420-5 • $16.99

The Power in Cubase: Tracking Audio, MIDI, and Virtual Instruments
by Matthew Loel T. Hepworth
Softcover w/DVD-ROM • 978-1-4584-1366-6 • $16.99

Mixing and Mastering with Cubase
by Matthew Loel T. Hepworth
Softcover w/DVD-ROM • 978-1-4584-1367-3 • $16.99

HAL•LEONARD®

Prices, contents, and availability subject to change without notice.

0312